THE
PRESENCE
CENTERED
CHURCH

BILL ELLIFF

The Presence-Centered Church

Copyright © 2015
Bill Elliff

TruthInk Publications
6600 Crystal Hill Road
North Little Rock, AR
USA

Editing: Andy Scheer

Cover and interior design: Keith Runkle

All rights reserved. No part of this publication may be reproduced, stored in retrieval systems, or transmitted in any form or by any means—electronic, mechanical, photocopying, recording, or otherwise—without prior written permission of the publisher.

All Scripture quotations, unless otherwise indicated, are taken from the New American Standard Bible®, Copyright © 1960, 1962, 1963, 1968, 1971, 1972, 1973, 1975, 1977, 1995 by The Lockman Foundation. Used by permission. (www.Lockman.org)

Scripture quotations marked Williams are from the Williams New Testament, The New Testament in the Language of the People, by Charles B. Williams. Copyright © 1937; renewed 1965, 1966, 1986 by Edith S. Williams. Copyright 1995 by Charlotte Williams Sprawls. Used by permission.

ISBN: 978-0-9831168-1-3

Printed in the United States of America by TruthInk Publications

Dedicated to the pioneers of
The Summit Church
in North Little Rock, Arkansas,
who launched into the deep, November 1, 1998,
with a passionate desire to build a church
where our gracious God and needy people
would be pleased to dwell.

FOREWORD

If you are content to live without revival, you will.

When I heard the late revivalist Leonard Ravenhill issue this passionate plea for revival, I had no idea that just a short time later a young seminary graduate would be lying prostrate on the floor of my office crying out to God, "Lord, I want revival more than I want to breathe."

Something inside of me couldn't escape the radical, holy desire of these two men. It was as if God Himself were issuing a purpose statement for my life, and for all those who love His glory. These encounters, plus one other, set in motion how I would spend the rest of my life.

The other experience is difficult to describe—almost too wonderful to put into words. All I can say is that I tasted the manifest presence of God in revival. In a little town in Indiana, I smelled the fire. I heard the wind. I witnessed churches transformed. I watched lives dramatically, instantaneously change. I caught a glimpse of God's glory. Unmistakably, God came to town. And the town came to God. And I will never be the same. The manifest presence of God drew me like a magnet to surrender my life to something I could no longer live without: genuine revival.

And I've spent the remainder of my adult life seeking to help believers and churches cultivate the presence of Christ. Having seen the fire, the smoke is forever on my clothes.

That's why I'm thrilled to be writing the foreword for this book. Bill Elliff has years of experience leading congregations into the presence of God as a pastor and revivalist. Through years of practice and reflection, Bill has become one of the foremost experts in the country regarding how to systematically create congregational contexts that are conducive for God to move in the hearts of people.

Even more importantly, Bill was there when the church he pastored experienced a dramatic and prolonged season of revival. What began with an unexpected but powerful Sunday morning service that flowed over the boundaries of their normal multiple service format well into the afternoon—then turned into weeks of consecutive nightly meetings, startling levels of open confession, scores of conversions, and thousands of dollars freely given to meet needs and advance the gospel. When Bill gives the principles and pathways for a Presence-centered church, he speaks of what he has seen in the trenches of church life.

In recent years, Bill's church has freed up a large portion of his time to help churches everywhere experience genuine revival and spiritual awakening. He serves nationally with the OneCry movement as a speaker and author. And he has dedicated his life to the fulfillment of the vision that is expressed in this book.

Virtually everything has been tried in American church life. We have access to the best equipment, the best programs, the best advice, the best consultations. But the one thing that makes the difference is rarely pursued as the primary matter of utmost urgency. Yet that factor—the extraordinary presence and power of Christ through outpourings of the Holy Spirit—is what is vitally missing in order to fulfill the church's extraordinary mission in the 21st century.

As you read this revival manifesto for churches that has been forming in Bill Elliff's soul for more than four decades, I pray that a longing for revival will grip your imagination and shape your plans for your own congregation. Revival is not only possible, it can be pursued corporately. With this book, the whole church has a wise and ready-made guide.

Byron Paulus
President/Executive Director of
Life Action Ministries

Founder of the OneCry Movement

As You Begin . . .

If you are reading this book, you are probably interested in Christ's bride, the Church. But like me, you may be deeply concerned for her (particularly the American church) as you see her current state. I want you to dream with me for a moment. Imagine a church . . .

- Where God is clearly and consistently present and the evidence is unmistakable not only to you, but also to the world around you. Where every gathering—large or small—is evaluated with one question: Was God there?

- Where worship is so accessible, authentic, and powerful that people are thrilled and overwhelmed with Christ. Where they are not focused on the style of worship, but the beauty of Christ. Where church members run, not to be entertained or seen, but to worship God in "spirit and truth."

- Where week after week the truths of God are clearly presented and quickened to people's hearts, and they feel they have heard from God Himself. Where the Word of God is honored through aggressive obedience.

- Where the altars are regularly filled and the homes of the members are filled with people responding to God.

- Where unbelievers' hearts are pierced and they are crying out, "What must I do to be saved?" And daily people are being added to the church.

- Where the whole church carries a great burden for the world, and the church is clearly on God's mission.

- Where the worst sinner feels so loved he can't leave, but so confronted he can't stay where he is.

- Where children are intentionally discipled by their parents, and the church is their greatest partner in the process.

3

- Where students are so enamored with their parents' spiritual experience, that they are drawn to Christ. Where they are being equipped in ways that prepare them for life so when they leave home, they do not fall away from the Lord.

- Where people are being visibly changed into the likeness of Christ. Where they look, walk, and talk like Him. And where their constant burden and highest joy is to disciple others.

- Where people are so generous in their giving, there is no more need among those who attend.

- Where vibrant, God-filled community is available for anyone.

- Where gossip, slander, and disunity are a distant memory.

- Where people are meeting with God daily and they know how to get their soul happy in Jesus.

- Where prayer is unceasing and is becoming the atmosphere in which people live and breathe.

- Where people are excited to come to a prayer meeting because they know that prayer accelerates the movement of God.

- Where God's love flows in unceasing acts of service. Where there are more volunteers than places of ministry.

- Where backsliding Christians are quickly confronted with such love and grace that repentance is the norm, not the exception. Where believers are continual, humble, glad repenters who live with the joy of God's salvation.

- Where loving cooperation is experienced among the congregations in a city and there is an obvious spirit of unity. Where there is completion, not competition, and the diversity of the church is celebrated, with no compromise to the primary truths of the Word of God.

- Where God is calling and sending church members all around the world to reach people and plant churches.

- Where more is done outwardly than inwardly, and there is a healthy balance of these two dynamics.

- Where the kingdom of God is rapidly advancing and the devil is retreating.

- Where there is undeniable joy!

The church you've just dreamed of (and may have been envisioning for many years) is a church where God is present. Where He is manifesting Himself and making Himself known.

More than a dream, this is God's deep desire. It is what the Great Architect has designed for His family. It permeates the DNA of the body He is building to reach needy people and advance His kingdom. It's not meant to be imagined, but experienced. God desires this authentic possibility even more than you do. He is knocking at the door.

I know very little compared to what some may know about God's presence. But I have experienced enough to long for more . . . and I know there is more for us all. It would be my highest honor if somehow this small book would help Christ's church fling wide the door to Him. Like Tozer, "If my fire is not large it is yet real, and there may be those who can light their candle at its flame."[1]

Bill Elliff
July 2015
The West Barn
North Little Rock, AR

[1] A.W. Tozer, "The Pursuit of God," (Christian Publications, Camp Hill, Penn., 1982), pg. 9

CONTENTS

1 🎵

THE DOOR

> "When the Lord divided Canaan among the tribes of Israel,
> Levi received no share of the land. God said to him simply,
> 'I am thy part and thine inheritance,' and by those words
> made him richer than all his brethren, richer than all the
> kings and rajas who have ever lived in the world . . . the
> man who has God for his treasure has all things in One.[1]
>
> A.W. Tozer

Imagine a door. Behind it are some incredible gifts with your name on them, and you are invited to enter. Would you be curious?

What if someone told you a new car awaited you behind the door? Would you reach for the knob?

What if, behind that door, lay the title to your dream home, as a gift? Would you run to see what's on the other side?

What if there was a suitcase with millions of dollars, just for the taking?

But imagine still more. What if behind that door was all the wisdom you would ever need for every decision of life . . . or all the knowledge about everything you needed . . . or a perfect love that would give you a passion for God and others? Or the grace to face any circumstance with integrity and joy? Or the power to do everything you would be called to do for the rest of your life?

Would you enter?

There is such a door and such a promise. For Christ Himself has made it possible to enter into His presence. He is both door and reward! The great treasure is not earthly possessions, but Christ Himself. And in His presence is "fullness of joy" and at His right hand are "pleasures forever" (Psalm 16:11)!

No earthly treasure can really compare to the riches of His presence. All of the wisdom, knowledge, and love you need (and abundantly more) is available when you are experiencing Him, because everything flows from the presence of the Lord. Everything. If you have Him, you have all you will ever need or want.

This also means that without this presence you are bankrupt. You are a mere human, doomed to a life of meager power, little love, and insufficient means. All the world can offer will never satisfy. All you can give others are your best thoughts and limited abilities, all severely damaged by the fall of man. But if you are experiencing the presence, you have all that God has, for you have Him. This . . . is a very important door.

Everything flows from the presence of the Lord. Everything

THE POVERTY OF LOST PRESENCE

Our First Parents walked away from that door. Tempted by the one who had been banished from God's presence (and who loves company), they were deceived into believing life without God would be better. Ignoring God's clear directions, they made their own decisions and became the lord of their own lives. They never suspected they were losing their most important gift.

When the Lord came looking for them, they "hid themselves from the presence of the LORD God among the trees of the garden" (Genesis 3:8). (Imagine trying to hide yourself from the God who made both you and the garden!) Not only had they lost God's presence, but their shame also stripped them of the desire to be with Him.

We would hope that Adam and Eve were just an aberration, but their son, Cain, learned well from his parents. The lack of God's rule in his life led to anger and murder and then he too "went out from the presence of the LORD" (Genesis 4:16). And on and on it has gone through human history. There could be no greater loss . . . for everything flows from the presence of the Lord.

> *God formed us for His pleasure, and so formed us that we, as well as He, can, in divine communion, enjoy the sweet and mysterious mingling of kindred personalities. He meant us to see Him and live with Him and draw our life from His smile. But we have been guilty of that "foul revolt" of which Milton speaks when describing the rebellion of Satan and his hosts.*
>
> *We have broken with God. We have ceased to obey Him or love Him, and in guilt and fear have fled as far as possible from His presence . . . So the life of man upon the earth is a life away from the Presence, wrenched loose from that "blissful center" which is our right and proper dwelling place, our first estate which we kept not, the loss of which is the cause of our unceasing restlessness."[2]*

THE HAVES AND HAVE-NOTS

Humanity is divided into two groups: those who experience God's intimate presence and those who do not. This is the world's clearest distinction. Look at the men and women of great biblical renown: Abraham, Joseph, Moses, David, Deborah, Esther, Elijah and Elisha, Mary, Peter, James and John, and the apostle Paul. What made them extraordinary? What granted them open doors of service and powerful deeds? What made them distinct from others? What brought heaven to men on earth and took men from earth to heaven through their ministries? It was God's presence . . . for everything flows from the presence of the Lord.

LEADING ON EMPTY

Browse through the lives of great spiritual leaders. You will quickly see the defining difference was that God was with them.

Moses' greatest fear was the prospect of leading God's people without God's presence. In a moment of desperate intercession he pleaded with God:

> *If Your **presence** does not go with us, do not lead us*
> *up from here. For how then can it be known that I have*
> *found favor in Your sight, I and Your people? Is it not by*
> *Your going with us, so that we, I and Your people, may be*
> *distinguished from all the other people who are upon the*
> *face of the earth? (Exodus 33:15–16 emphasis added)*

It had taken 80 eighty years of training and brokenness, but Moses knew well that he had nothing with which to lead these people, if He didn't have God. No leadership skill, persuasive words, clever wisdom, sophisticated marketing, or strategic planning could accomplish what needed to be done. Moses needed God—and God alone. He knew this so deeply, it led to desperate prayer and full surrender. He would do anything to gain and maintain God's active presence.

The greatest earthly king who ever ruled Israel lived for the presence of God. When David was attacked, he realized that God was his only secure place of refuge.

> *You hide them in the secret place of Your **presence** from*
> *the conspiracies of man; You keep them secretly in a shelter*
> *from the strife of tongues. (Psalm 31:20 emphasis added)*

He understood God's presence was the source of "fullness of joy," and at God's right hand he would find "pleasures forever" (Psalm 16:11).

When David's soul languished, overwhelmed with the demands of life, he ran to God's presence. He knew it was his only source of help.

> *Why are you in despair, O my soul? And why have you*
> *become disturbed within me? Hope in God, for I shall*
> *again praise Him for the help of His **presence**. (Psalm 42:5*
> *emphasis added)*

David was a great king because he was humble and dependent. He knew where power and deliverance originated. His first and foremost principle of leadership was to rely on the presence.

> *For by their own sword they did not possess the land, and*
> *their own arm did not save them, but Your right hand and*

> *Your arm and the light of Your **presence**, for You favored them. (Psalm 44:3 emphasis added)*

David also knew he could never flee from God's presence (Psalm 139:7) and that the nearness of God was his greatest good (Psalm 73:28). Why were Moses and David such remarkable leaders? They understood the indispensible nature of God. They lived to experience Him and to help His people do the same. These seasons under Moses and David were the greatest times in Israel's history because of God's presence as both leaders and people cooperated with Him.

MADE FOR HIM

Souls who have tasted God's presence understand this and long for more. They know the difference of an environment filled with God. They are overwhelmed when God seems to manifest Himself in a worship service, while giving counsel to a friend, or when He graciously comes to them in the early morning hours. They have grasped that more can happen in five minutes of God's manifest presence than in fifty years of our best human efforts. They know the purpose of their lives, and of every common day, is to live and move and respond to the presence of the King!

> More can happen in five minutes of God's manifest presence than in fifty years of our best human efforts

We understand there are different measures of God's presence. God is omnipresent: everywhere at all times. There is the cultivated presence of God, as James encourages us to "draw near to God and He will draw near to you" (4:8). But what we long for and need is the manifest presence of God. Manifest means clearly seen, evident, undeniable. We seek the invasion of God in unique ways to do what only God can do.

In 1970 our nation was in the midst of a movement of God. It was not nationwide, as previous great awakenings, but it was an unusual stirring. Later called the Jesus Movement, it was highlighted by a visitation of God on the campus of Asbury College in Wilmore, Kentucky—a chapel service that lasted twenty-four hours a day for seven days and nights! A taste of this outpouring of God occurred on the college campus where I was a student in Arkansas. A fifteen-minute, student-led noonday service extended for over three hours. Confession, repentance, brokenness, and salvation occurred—with no orchestration except the leadership of the Holy Spirit. I had never seen such a flurry of God's activity.

As I experienced this moment of God's manifest presence, I cannot describe the sweetness and power of those days that followed. Even a struggling college student could see the difference. And that taste made me insatiably hungry for more.

Not long ago, I was gathered with fifty seasoned revival leaders from across America. When asked where they received their burden for spiritual awakening, well over half pointed to this period in the early '70s. What could have such a profound effect, changing the course of thousands of lives?

Nothing less than God's presence.

EXPANDED OPPORTUNITY

In the unfolding plan of our sovereign God, there came the moment when He expanded our ability to experience His presence. In the Old Testament, the Spirit came upon people at certain times for divine purposes. David, after his grievous sin, prayed, "Do not cast me away from Your presence and do not take your Holy Spirit from me" (Psalm 51:11).

But God always has more. Christ came to do His gracious work to provide pardon and cleansing to make us fit temples for Himself. After His ascension, He sent the promised Holy Spirit to dwell in all believers, never to leave. He promised to be with them and in them and all who believe (John 14:16–17).

The day of Pentecost ushered in this new age. Much like Jesus' birth, it was a spectacular display of God's presence. This was the beginning of the next chapter. The Spirit would now come to live in all believers. This allowed them, as they cooperated with Him, the incredible capacity to experience Him continually.

The days of the early church were filled with amazing phenomena. Love was undeniable, power was transforming and constant, and forgiveness was stunning—even toward their enemies. Boldness took common men and women and made them unrelenting champions for God's kingdom.

Giving was so hilariously generous, there actually came a moment among the 50,000-plus believers in Jerusalem that there was "no more need!" (Can you imagine that happening in your city?)

What turned this ragtag band of believers into a movement? A tidal wave of grace that swept across the known world with such power that all its enemies could not contain it? The Presence.

When two of the early church's leaders were imprisoned, the authorities that questioned them were amazed. The men in chains were "uneducated and untrained men. " Yet they marveled at Peter and John's wisdom and were taken aback by their boldness. The only explanation they could muster was that they had "been with Jesus" (Acts 4:13). For these early disciples, the recognizable difference was God's presence within them.

THE ENEMY'S DISTRACTIONS

Satan's greatest fear is the presence of God. When God shows up in power, Satan must flee—not just walk away, but run. So he continually tempts us to do anything that will abort God's presence. He infected the fledgling church. We see this as early as Acts 5, as a husband and wife let their desire for recognition pollute the stream of the church's generosity. God's judgment was quick and lethal, indicating He wanted to show the world an undefiled picture of what His manifest presence could do. This early church was to be a template for future generations of what church could and should be like.

As time ran on, the pull of the world, the flesh, and the devil invaded the growing church. Paul wrote letters to correct heresy, sinful behavior, and conflict—all things that indicate God's absence. The Corinthians were so swept away in their sinfulness, Paul leveled the greatest possible indictment: they were acting like "mere men," looking to their own ability and not the Spirit's power (1 Corinthians 3:1–3). Although God was available, so were the idols of the world. Their idolatry was quenching the Spirit's movement among them.

DIVINE INVASIONS

Not willing to let us slide into mere humanity—and driven by a perfect love that has come to seek and to save that which was lost—throughout history God has graciously interrupted our lethargy with heavenly invasions of His presence.

Personally

Although every believer has the Spirit, it is possible to know about Him, even to have previously experienced His presence, but fail to walk in a vibrant relationship with Him. When the believer is living without this conscious sense of Christ, he is missing the most joyful part of living and the only real power for effectiveness.

Charles Haddon Spurgeon (who believed in the continual indwelling of the Holy Spirit) wrote of his experiences of Christ's presence as "visits in the night."

> *For our Lord to visit us is something more than for us to have the assurance of our salvation, although that is very delightful, and none of us would be satisfied unless we possessed it. To know that Jesus loves me is one thing, but to be visited by Him in love is much more.*
>
> *Nor it is simply a close contemplation of Christ, for we can picture Him as exceedingly fair and majestic and yet not have Him consciously near us. As delightful and instructive as it is to behold the likeness of Christ by meditation, the enjoyment of His actual presence is something more.*
>
> *The actual, though spiritual, coming of Christ is what we so much desire . . . By spiritual we do not mean unreal. In fact, the spiritual is what is most real to spiritual men. I believe in the true and real presence of Jesus with His people, for such a presence has been real to my spirit.*[3]

God longs for us to experience Him intimately and continually. He gladly makes Himself known in every believing heart that turns to Him in humble dependence and genuine surrender. He has promised that if we draw near to Him, He will draw near to us (James 4:8). What true believer has not known moments in a worship service, a quiet time out in God's creation, or in a moment of prayer or ministry when God has been unusually evident? God longs for that to be our daily experience.

God's presence can become so real that He makes the simplest moments beautiful. Early one morning during an incredible season of revival in the church I pastor, I was walking down a hallway. I realized I had not yet that morning consciously connected with Christ. "Good morning, Lord," I breathed in prayer. He then spoke to my heart, not audibly of course, but in a profound, wonderful way. He washed over my soul with the amazing personal love He had for me. It took my breath away to realize that He knew my name, that He would gladly condescend to address me, and that He would talk with me as friend to friend. I will never forget the joy of that one, simple moment. No agenda. Just God in loving communion with one of His children. The glorious birthright of every believer, this intimacy should be our common experience.

God places no limitation on His willingness to revive and intimately connect with individual hearts. Throughout Scripture He invites us to pursue Him. To every seeking, repentant heart, He promises a fresh experience of Himself. In the next chapter we will look more deeply at how to develop this personal intimacy.

Corporately
God graciously gives seeking churches moments of His heightened presence. Every church leader who is passionate for God has experienced some measure of this and longs for more! These are the wonderful mercy drops when people know that God has chosen to enter the room and make Himself known.

If we are not careful, we may miss these visitations or run past them, fearful of what an unloosed God might do to our comfortable "order of worship." But to the discerning soul, these are the moments and seasons we long to experience. If embraced, they can extend into mighty movements of God, sometimes lasting months and years.

Solomon Stoddard, the grandfather-in-law of Jonathan Edwards and a pastor himself, said he had known in his church three such seasons of the mighty movement of God's manifest presence. The leaders of

Stoddard's day understood such outpourings. When those moments were absent, they cried out for them. When they were present, leaders cooperated with God so He could accomplish all He desired in their midst.

In 2010, our church was longing for God. We fasted and prayed for months. On April 11, 2011, the Lord moved in power in a Sunday worship service, extending the meeting until 3 pm. People were saved, lives changed, glory seen. If that was all we experienced, it would have been a day we'd talk about for years.

But we sensed God wanted to do more, so we invited people to return the next night to our regular "First Monday" prayer meeting. The room was packed and the meeting again lasted three hours. There was deep repentance, many calls for prayer, and immediate provisions from God. Wedding rings and even a car were given to meet multiple needs. Thousands of dollars changed hands. A forty-year alcoholic was delivered (and remains so to this day). People's lives were gloriously healed of all kinds of spiritual maladies. Lost people came to Christ. Heaven came down.

We felt prompted to continue the next night and the next . . . and that invasion of God's presence extended for five weeks as we met every night for three to four hours except Saturday. Every single day people were spontaneously saved. We baptized people daily, many in their street clothes. We came to a point where, as far as we could determine, there was no more financial need among the people of the church because God had granted us the joyful freedom of liberality. When needs were mentioned, offering baskets were placed on the altar and they would quickly fill and be distributed to those who had needs.

Everywhere our people went they shared Christ with a boldness we had never seen. Ministries were started that continue to this day. Alcoholics and drug addicts were delivered. Everything we read about in Acts 2 was happening, in some measure. It was the purest, sweetest, most effortless season of ministry I've ever experienced.

How can we explain such a time? It was simply the manifest presence of God, blessing us with a vivid reminder of who He is and what He can do. Those days lifted our passion and faith to a new level and we have never been the same.

We know in a new way that everything flows from the presence of the Lord. If you have Him, you have all you need—and more.

Nationwide Outpourings

In the most glorious invasions, there are seasons when God makes Himself known on a nationwide level. We call these revivals when they descend upon the church and awakenings when they bring lost men and women to life.

In the first 150 years of America's existence, we experienced such movements every thirty to fifty years. The First Great Awakening, The Second Great Awakening, The Prayer Revival of 1857–1858, and the worldwide impact of the Welsh Revival of 1904–1905 ushered millions into the kingdom in a matter of months. Although God used men and women, no single person could receive glory for these outpourings because of their magnitude.

Many books speak of these great movements. My dear friend and colleague, Byron Paulus, and I sought to describe some of this in the book *OneCry: A Nationwide Call for Spiritual Awakening*.[4] We outline the desperate need for us to unite in fervent, sustained prayer for revival and awakening.

Every spiritual historian would agree that these invasions are nothing less than the manifest visitation of the presence of God. Pastor, revivalist, and historian Richard Owen Roberts said that real revival can be defined in one word: "God!"

> These are seasons when God reminds us in broad strokes what heaven is like.

These are seasons when God reminds us in broad strokes what heaven is like. The church has been called to pray and work so God's kingdom will come and His will be done on earth as it is being done right now in heaven (Matthew 6:10). We forget (or have never comprehended) what heaven is like. During seasons of revival, we see a bit of heaven.

We bask in the beauty of Jesus, gladly reject our idols, and worship Him alone. We witness the power of the Spirit and believe Him for great things. We embrace the sovereignty of God, lay aside our petty issues, and grow up to be bigger Christians. We unite in God's mission and boldly join His agenda to make disciples of all nations, baptizing them and teaching them to observe all the things He has commanded (Matthew 28:19–20).

Divine, nationwide invasions give us critical course corrections. Without them, we begin to compare ourselves with ourselves, vainly thinking our human plans and results are all God wants. We become satisfied with our pitiful status quo. We grow proud of our work (believing it is what we have done) and claim the credit.

During revival, God blows all our silliness away like chaff. He lifts our vision to remind us He can do "far more abundantly beyond all that we ask or think" (Ephesians 3:20). We see the "much more" of God. We humbly recognize that the endgame of this invasion is so He alone can again receive "glory in the church and in Christ Jesus to all generations forever and ever" (Ephesians 3:21). And we realize it is all from Him, for Him, by Him, and through Him.

Personally, corporately, and nationally, the greatest moments of our existence—and the greatest movements for the kingdom—happen when God manifests Himself, when His presence is clearly seen and felt.

> *The world is perishing for lack of the knowledge of God and the Church is famishing for want of His presence. The instant cure of most of our religious ills would be to enter the Presence in spiritual experience, to become suddenly aware that we are in God and that God is in us. This would lift us out of our pitiful narrowness and cause our hearts to be enlarged."*[5]

OUR PASSION
So what kind of person do you want to be and what kind of church do you want? More important, what do you think God wants?

Are you content with a business-as-usual church? Church that can be explained? Church that is accomplishing only what human hands can build? Church that has to entertain? Church that relies on the next slick marketing tool to attract a lost world?

Or do you long for "far more abundantly beyond? "The"much more" of God? A movement that comes from His presence?

THE PRESENCE-CENTERED CHURCH

Many pastors have written about models for building God's church. I have benefitted from most. None of us has all the truth. But like a group of blind men trying to describe an elephant, we each touch on different sides of this massive movement called the church.

Hopefully this book can fuel our burden to see the church flourish and expand for God's glory. This discussion will focus on God's presence and encourage us to do everything necessary to build a church where God is pleased to dwell. To make it our supreme passion to invite God into every corner of our experience. To let the constant, ruthless evaluation of our work be,"Is God here?"

We need this. Sadly, something is missing in the church. For all our good intentions, each year thousands of churches close their doors (most studies say over 6,000 a year). Hundreds of pastors leave the ministry every month, and more than 75 percent of American churches are not growing. Although there are many wonderful, vibrant churches, our nation's moral and spiritual condition shows the effects of a weakened church. We are having little effect on society and society is having a massive effect on us. We have crossed a tipping point. No political manipulation can bring our nation back from the spiritual wasteland we are entering.

We need God. We need Him deeply and desperately. And we need Him now. Without a divine invasion of His manifest presence, every life, every local church, and the church in our nation is doomed to meager impact and overall decline.

Let us make it the goal of our lives and ministries to do everything God directs to discover His presence: in our lives, our churches, and our nation. To center our existence as a church around that goal. To prepare a highway for our God. To create environments where He can manifest Himself. To get the roadways ready, then cry out for His invasion.

The following pages define some of the broad strokes. It will take some work. But it's worth the price because *everything flows from the presence of the Lord!*

1. A.W. Tozer, The Pursuit of God, (Camp Hill, Penn.: Christian Publications, 1982), 18.
2. A.W. Tozer, The Pursuit of God, 35.
3. Charles H. Spurgeon, Joy in Christ's Presence, (New Kensington, Penn.: Whitaker House, 1997), 13.
4. Byron Paulus and Bill Elliff, OneCry: A Call for Spiritual Awakening, (Chicago: Moody Publishers, 2014).
5. A.W. Tozer, The Pursuit of God, 53.

2

ENTER FIRST

> "Both Scripture and experience teach that it is we, not God, who determine the degree of intimacy with Him that we enjoy. We are at this moment as close to God as we really choose to be. True, there are times when we would like to know a deeper intimacy, but when it comes to the point, we are not prepared to pay the price involved . . . Everything in our Christian life and service flows from our relationship with God."[1]
>
> J. Oswald Sanders

I went three years before I really noticed the cute girl who sat behind me in the ninth grade. Then on a crisp, fall day, I suddenly became aware of Holly Hicks. She had grown up.

It didn't take me long to strike up a conversation. In a matter of weeks we were sitting together at a church meeting. Before long I was smitten. Head-over-heels.

My approach might be different than yours, but at that point I did not visit the library to see what I could learn about Holly. I didn't search the internet. (We didn't *have* the internet then, or home computers!) I didn't simply want to know a few facts about this girl. I wanted to be with her—all the time! And the more I was around her, the more I wanted to be around her. Which has led me to being around her for more than forty-three years!

WITH HIM

In two verses, Mark's Gospel records the heartbeat of Jesus' ministry with His disciples. Jesus was building the first church. He knew what was needed so it would last until He returned.

His approach was very different than our ideas of highly programmed ministry, although there is nothing wrong with some of those forms. He didn't disciple the twelve by meeting them once a week on a Tuesday night or deciding to read a book or two.

> *He appointed twelve, so that they would* **be with Him** *and that He could send them out to preach and to have authority to cast out the demons. (Mark 3:14–15 emphasis added)*

For Jesus, discipleship was about His presence with those He had chosen and loved. That they would "be with Him." Jesus knew that the greatest gift, and the most important experience and training, would come as His followers spent time in His presence. The result would be proclaiming the gospel of the kingdom and taking back ground from the Evil One. But it began and was sustained by His presence.

Jesus would remind His disciples that the secret to bearing abundant, remaining fruit for His kingdom was abiding in Him (John 15). The English word "abide" is the verb form of "abode," a dwelling place. What a beautiful thought that we should make our home in Him. God's plan is to reside in us, and for us to make our home in Him.

> For Jesus, discipleship was about His presence with those He had chosen and loved.

The apostle Paul caught this. He reminds the Corinthians with stark simplicity of the goal of their high calling.

> *God is faithful, through whom you were called into fellowship with His Son, Jesus Christ our Lord.* *(1 Corinthians 1:9)*

Our first and highest task is to be in fellowship with Jesus Christ. This word implies the sharing of common life: an authentic, connected, experience in the presence of Jesus. Not just learning about Him, but living with Him intimately.

Paul further illustrates this when he lists all his human accomplishments, then says they are meaningless to him now. His one desire was to "know Him," and he gave this goal all his attention (Philippians 3).

LEADERS LEAD

If you are a leader in your church and you long for a Presence-Centered church, it begins with your life. You may be a senior pastor, elder, staff member, small-group leader, youth or children's worker... but whatever your capacity, you are important. If you have any hope for others to enter God's presence and dwell there, you must first be willing to pay the price to enter yourself. Others may not follow your lead (that's a whole different book).[2] But they will certainly not go there if you don't. The foundation of a Presence-Centered church is a core of leaders who know how to live and move in intimate fellowship with Jesus.

There is a price. Many leaders have boasted of their passion for Christ, their hunger to see Him move in their church. But when the moment for stepping into vital connection with Jesus comes, they have made no adjustments in their life to experience Christ personally. At times, all of us have experienced this tragic failure.

A leader who really wants God's manifest presence in his church and community will first seek God's presence in his own life. God rarely bypasses this principle. That's a strong truth, but there's also a strong promise. Our revealing God has said that whoever seeks Him will find Him, for He is not hiding (2 Chronicles 15:2).

God makes many promises about His availability. He wants to be known even more than you want to know Him. We know this because He's perfect in His affections. We drift in and out of passion. But God always wants to express His love to His children and He longs for them to experience more of Him.

A mature leader desires a growing, vibrant, daily experience with God. Great men know they need this and they have learned how to get there. So what does it take to become a Presence-Centered leader?

Daily Time

Life consists of common, daily moments. Men who want to experience God don't squander these precious opportunities. With authentic humility and growing wisdom, they determine to seek His presence daily and early. Everyone must find their own rhythm for the best time to meet with Him. But many great men and women emulate Jesus, who went out "in the early morning, while it was still dark" to enjoy the mornings with God before the day's activities began (Mark 1:35).

George Mueller, the spiritual giant who had such mighty effect for the kingdom, discovered this secret.

> *While I was staying at Nailsworth, it pleased the Lord to teach me a truth, irrespective of human instrumentality, as far as I know, the benefit of which I have not lost, though now . . . more than forty years have since passed away.*
>
> *The point is this: I saw more clearly than ever, that the first great and primary business to which I ought to attend every day was, to have my soul happy in the Lord. The first thing to be concerned about was not, how much I might serve the Lord, how I might glorify the Lord; but how I might get my soul into a happy state, and how my inner man might be nourished.*
>
> *I scarcely ever suffer now in this way. For my heart being nourished by the truth, being brought into experimental fellowship with God, I speak to my Father, and to my Friend (vile though I am, and unworthy of it!) about the things that He has brought before me in His precious Word.*[3]

Mueller entered into this "experimental fellowship" daily. He would walk in his yard every morning, reading the Scriptures and meditating and praying through them until he found joy. He *entered into* God's presence. As a result, his ministry was filled with the irresistible aroma of God.

This was the experience in the 1600's of Madame Guyon, who influenced Fenelon, Count Von Zinzendorf, John Wesley, Hudson Taylor and others. She would concentrate on a small portion of Scripture and pray it in deeply in an earnest passion to enter God's presence and experience Him.[4] The point of her daily, continuous prayer was not to get things, but to experience Him who is the Source of all that matters and lasts. She moved from a belief in merely a time of prayer, to continuous, unceasing prayer throughout the day. She wrote in one poem, "There was a period when I chose, a time and place for prayer, But now I seek that constant prayer, in inward stillness known."[5]

Many days we read the news, watch television, talk to others, and waste time along the way. Perhaps the greatest key to King David's intimacy with God was his refusal to put anything before His eyes that would divert His attention from the Lord. "I will set no worthless thing before my eyes. I hate the work of those who fall away. It shall not fasten its grip on me" (Psalm 101:3). We may feel some mindless indulgence is not wrong. But we must evaluate carefully. Is it worthless? Will it divert me from the most important activity? What a tragedy if we stand before God one day, and His indictment to us is, "Could you not watch with me for one hour?" (Matthew 26:40).

On a practical note, I believe the Lord will wake you in the morning when He desires, if you'll cooperate with Him. I am often awakened early and I simply ask the Lord in prayer, "Do you want me to get up now?" If I sense the answer is yes, I get up. I have learned that almost invariably something from God is waiting for me.

Without question, the richest hours of my life have been the "visits in the night" with Him. What an honor to sit at the feet of the King of Kings! I'm not trying to sound mystical, but this has proven true in my experience and those of many others.

A dear friend has not set an alarm for twenty years, relying on the Lord to get him up when needed and cooperating with Him whenever He calls. Bill McLeod, the pastor God so greatly used in the Canadian revival, told the Lord that every night He would awaken him to pray for revival, he would get up and pray. The Lord did awaken Him (and McLeod cooperated) every night for over thirty years!

Extended Time

As Jesus developed His first church, He set in place another pattern. He would often steal away for extended time in the presence of the Father.

> *It was at this time that He went off to the mountain to pray, and He spent the whole night in prayer to God. (Luke 6:12)*

I have often wondered at our arrogance about this. If the Son of God needed extended hours with the Father, how do we think we could do otherwise and minister effectively? Our lives are filled with activity, appointments, and hundreds of conversations, but it is our pride that causes us to rarely give God times of undivided attention.

> If the Son of God needed extended hours with the Father, how do we think we could do otherwise and minister effectively?

Right now, all around you, people are talking and music is playing. All you have to do to access this barrage is turn on a radio and tune it to the right channel. But you'll never hear it unless you're dialed to the proper frequency. The same is true with God.

> *There is hardly ever a complete silence in our soul. God is whispering to us well nigh incessantly. Whenever the sounds of the world die out in the soul, or sink low, then we hear these whisperings of God. He is always whispering to us, only we do not always hear because of the noise, hurry, and distraction which life causes as it rushes on.[6]*

Any leader who desires to experience the presence must take deliberate time to dial in. Go to a cabin, an outdoor place, or a quiet room in your local library. There's something very important about leaving your normal environment, especially going into the nature God has created. Spend the entire day with Christ. Read whole books of the Bible.

Ask God what He wants to say to you. Journal what He is revealing. Turn your phone off and use your computer only to access Bible tools. Usually you will make more progress in this one day of concentrated communion than in a whole week of scattered thinking.

Develop a rhythm of regular retreats. Be with Him . . . and listen. Hear God and discover His presence. Have no agenda for such days except Him!

If you think you don't have time, begin by repenting of your opinion of your own importance. The world can make it without you one day a month. And many would benefit from your becoming a leader who is regularly entering the presence of Christ.

Fasting

Life is loud. Our minds run constantly, our emotions drive us, and our wills battle for control. There is nothing like fasting to quiet us and take us into the Lord's presence.

In a time of extended fasting, Psalm 35:13 became very real to me as the psalmist said, "I humbled my soul with fasting." Fasting quiets the soul: the mind, will, and emotions. It says "no" to what is in you that is always clamoring for more. You experience an amazing quiet when the voices that pull you in multiple directions are starved and silenced.

The first few days of fasting I'm usually just plain mad! I enjoy eating, so depriving myself of what I love is a battle (which tells me, on many levels, why it is so important). But after the initial shock, fasting settles me in. It seems to help me hear God in a way that nothing else will accomplish. My mind is sharper, my spiritual senses more attuned. If I am pursuing Him (not pursuing a fast, human recognition, or lesser reasons), He is eager to meet with me.

If you feel distant and distracted, spend a day or multiple days giving attention to nothing but Him—and see what you experience in His presence. Jesus did not say in Matthew 6:16, "If you happen to fast" but "when you fast," assuming it would be a routine part of our spiritual life. If you are facing a big decision, fasting offers incredible benefits. There are multiple ways to fast. The key is to fast from whatever God directs. It could be food, media, entertainment, or something else.

Walk away from the noise, the programs, the busy-ness. "The simplicity which is in Christ is rarely found among us," Tozer said. "In its stead are programs, methods, organizations and a world of nervous activities which occupy time and attention but can never satisfy the longing of the heart."[7] Get still and pursue the one thing that matters and lasts.

Unceasing Prayer

I have been captured the past few years by three simple words that frame a command in 1 Thessalonians 5:17 that most of us feel is impossible:"Pray without ceasing." For years I gave this little thought. But during the season of revival in our church, many of us began to realize that this was not only possible, but essential.

God will not make any demand on our lives that we can't accomplish by His grace. If He says to forgive, we can forgive with His empowering. I may not know the way, but there is a way—and I will find it if I pursue Him.

Our Great Intercessor commands us to join Him in pray without interruption. So we should make it the great quest of our lives to pray all day long. To come to the place where we are moving in the atmosphere of continual communion with God.

Our great mistake is that we see prayer formally: something done before meals or meetings. Prayer is shorthand for talking with God. If we believe He is around us and in us, then prayer without ceasing becomes possible.

"Pray without ceasing" becomes a verse of conviction. Do I realize I am in God's presence? Do I remember He is here and cares deeply about everything that happens in my life? Am I willing to listen to Him right now, letting Him join the conversation of my life, to speak whatever He desires?

Begin by cultivating the practice of praying about everything. When you need to give an answer, pray. When you are making a decision, pray. When you are having a conversation, pray. When your mind is in neutral, thank God in prayer. Before a phone call, pray. Pray before every event of your day—and during every event. To pray without ceasing means simply to let Him into every moment. George Mueller, who recorded over 40,000 answers to his prayers, said:

> *I live in the spirit of prayer. I pray as I walk about, when I lie down and when I rise up. And the answers are always*

> *coming. Thousands and tens of thousands of times have my
> prayers been answered. When once I am persuaded that a
> thing is right and for the glory of God, I go on praying for
> it until the answer comes.*[8]

We view prayer as a separate compartment, as something for a select few or an activity we should do occasionally as needed. But communion with Christ lies at the heart of our relationship with Christ. We can survive without a finger, an arm, or a leg. But we cannot live without our heart.

How can we expect to live rightly if we fail to commune with Jesus all day long? If we are praying, we are *with Him* and receiving all that comes from His presence.

Spiritual Examination

Drifting is easy. The tyranny of the urgent and the routine demands of life, combined with our leanings toward sin and the temptations of the Enemy, pull us away from God's presence. Paul feared this for the Corinthian church.

> *But I am afraid that, as the serpent deceived Eve by his
> craftiness, your minds will be led astray from the simplicity
> and purity of devotion to Christ.* (2 Corinthians 11:3)

Jesus examines our lives all the time. The owner of the vineyard constantly watches over His vines—pruning, caring, and working to produce more fruit and enduring fruit. When needed, He comes directly to us as He did to the seven churches in Revelation and gives specifics about what is aborting our walk with Him and our effectiveness with others.

If we fail to take regular moments to listen to His evaluation and examine our lives, we will be lulled into thinking we are in good spiritual condition. We can easily become self-deceived. If we want to experience Christ's presence and lead others there, we should be the first on the examination table. We must take time to listen to the Lord regarding our spiritual health. We should let Him put a spiritual stethoscope to our hearts and give us not only a diagnosis, but also fresh prescriptions to return us to health.

We must repent from every sin that is hindering God's presence and clear our consciences with those we've wronged. Go all the way to the bottom and let the Holy Spirit reveal the groundwork of our heart. Spiritual examination is useless without spiritual surrender. We must turn from our sin and turn to Christ or we will be like the man James speaks of who looks at his face in the mirror, possibly seeing his hair out of place, then walks away, forgets what he has seen, and makes no adjustment (James 1:23–25).

For years I carried the small tract in my Bible, "Not I, But Christ." It helps me to regularly review this spiritual checklist, which is reprinted in Appendix B. In Appendix C you'll find a simple evaluation tool for leaders from the pastoral epistles (1 and 2 Timothy and Titus) called "Fifty Marks of a Man of God." It would do your soul good to study those pages and regularly take a deliberate time of evaluation with these tools.

Honest Accountability

Years ago my pastor father suffered a deep moral and spiritual fall. It was devastating to all of us and especially to him. In the end, God brought him to great repentance, but the damage it caused was monumental.[9]

The startling thing to me and to most who knew him was that he was one of the godliest men we knew. But a small crack in his armor, combined with a harbored hurt, led to despair—and sin was crouching at the door. One thing came to me with great clarity: If my godly dad could fall, I could fall.

I became so fearful of this that I called three pastor buddies and asked them to join me in a retreat for the sole purpose of getting open and honest. I wanted to have some men in my life who would ask me the tough questions and speak lovingly and strongly to me about anything that might abort God's presence. Our first retreat was a revealing time of confession and transparency. It helped us remove the boulders in our lives that were blocking God's presence.

Honest accountability before trusted friends is essential for our spiritual health.

We met this year for our twentieth annual retreat. These men have saved my life on multiple occasions. We now talk weekly, not by some regimen, but because our lives are intertwined. We have learned that honest accountability before trusted friends is essential for our spiritual health.

It's easy to put on a façade. To fool people. To be so spiritually house-trained that you know how to sit up, roll over, and still play "leader" when your soul has drifted far from intimacy with Christ. But if you want to be a Presence-Centered leader, give access in your life to God's Word and to others filled with God's Word.

United Prayer

If your goal is to be used by God to build a church where He is pleased to dwell, not only must you live in God's presence, but your key leaders must also enter. It is a great privilege to have a leadership team filled with men and women unified in their passion for the presence of God. But it is not easy to get there. Sometimes we inherit staff members who are not on board. After months or years of coaching, they may still be unwilling to authentically pursue God's presence. Deal with this graciously but firmly.

This says something about how we find staff members and leaders. I've been helped by the Three "C's" of hiring. We must find people who have character, competence, and chemistry with the existing leaders. But we have added a fourth "C": culture. To become unified as a team, leaders must understand the culture we seek to develop and be in sync with the direction we believe the Lord is giving. For us, that must be a culture that seeks, above all else, the presence and glory of God.

Years ago I learned an amazing lesson about how to develop this unity. A group of pastors in our city began to meet for prayer at the Mayor's request because of the terrible condition of our inner city. We were greatly helped by our monthly prayer times together. We felt it was making a difference, so we decided to go on a four-day Pastor's Prayer Summit. It was four days of nothing but prayer, facilitated by two men from International Renewal Ministries who started the Pastor's Prayer Summit movement in the Northwest.

The first hours on Monday were fairly stilted. Men pontificated in prayer, some even re-preached in prayer their sermons from the day before! But in the afternoon, God graciously chose to enter the room. His presence became thick. Men began to get honest, confess their fears and inadequacies, and then pray for each other. Before the night was over, our souls had been knit together in a way we'd never experienced . . . and we had three more days to go! By Thursday I had twenty-five blood brothers in Christ who are my friends and colleagues to this day.

Much has happened as a result of this unity that could have happened no other way as we have continued our times in His presence for the past twenty years.

I learned that week (and it has been deeply reinforced since) that you cannot manufacture unity. Unity comes in the presence of the Lord, and the best way to accomplish this is to experience His presence in united prayer.

> You cannot manufacture unity. Unity comes in the presence of the Lord

Our Tuesday morning prayer times at our church with our pastoral team, Wednesday morning men's prayer, and our Thursday early morning prayer times with our elders are the most important hours of our week. I pray greatly in preparation for these times, asking God to bless us with His manifest presence and seeking His direction on how to help lead these times. These are also some of my primary opportunities to disciple young leaders.

Center these prayer times around what God is saying to you through His word. I agree with the great pastor and prayer leader Daniel Henderson, who often says that the best prayer is "Scripture-fed, Spirit-led, worship-based prayer!" People on your team may not know at first how to pray well. But after years of praying together, a rhythm and power will develop that will fuel your church. With our staff, we set no time limit on these meetings. There is a general idea, but we want the deck to be clear so that if God wants to take us deeper and longer, He can. It is His meeting and He is the leader.

Through the years, we have seen this simple practice of regular prayer among our leaders become the foundation for a Presence-Centered church. It is a wonderful way to build unity, discover the heart of God, and show new and young leaders what God's presence is all about. We are learning how to enter in together, then lead others there.

PAYING THE PRICE

Joshua had a great privilege. Moses had led the people across the wilderness, but Joshua would take them into the Promised Land. But the requirements were stiff. He needed to be in a position to hear God and move at God's slightest command.

> *This book of the law shall not depart from your mouth, but you shall meditate on it day and night, so that you may be careful to do according to all that is written in it; for then you will make your way prosperous, and then you will have success. (Joshua 1:8)*

God's instructions to Joshua centered on listening intentionally to the Lord and doing exactly as He said. Joshua discovered he must lead from God's presence.

Many men want the mantle of leadership without the price. But the cost is not a burden but a privilege, for the result is the presence from which comes everything good and perfect.

Do you want to build a Presence-Centered church? Then your personal experience of Him must be your highest priority. Nothing must get in the way. Everything must be built around this passion. You must enter first . . . and enter now.

> *It would seem that admission to the inner circle of deepening intimacy with God is the outcome of deep desire. Only those who count such intimacy a prize worth sacrificing anything else for are likely to attain it. If other intimacies are more desirable to us, we will not gain entry to that circle. The place on Jesus' breast is still vacant, and open to any who are willing to pay the price of deepening intimacy. We are now, and we will be in the future, only as intimate with God as we really choose to be.[10]*

1. J. Oswald Sanders, Enjoying Intimacy with God, (Chicago: Moody Press, 1980), 13–14.
2. Bill Elliff, Whitewater: Navigating the Rapids of Church Conflict, (Little Rock, Ark.: TruthInk Publications, 2009).
3. Cited in John Piper, Desiring God, (Colorado Springs, Colo.: Multnomah Books, 2011), 155–157
4. Madame Guyon, Experiencing the Depths of Jesus Christ, (Auburn, Me.: Seed Sowers Christian Books, 1981), 1–27.
5. http://christian-quotes.ochristian.com/Madame-Guyon-Quotes/
6. A.W. Tozer, quoting Fredrick Faber, Pursuit of God, (Camp Hill, Penn.: Christian Publications, 1982), 82.
7. A.W. Tozer, The Pursuit of God, 13.
8. An Hour with George Mueller, The Man of Faith to Whom God Gave Millions, by Charles R. Parsons; http://www.wholesomewords.org/biography/bmuller7.html
9. Read the whole story in Healing the Harbored Hurts of Your Heart by Bill Elliff.
10. J. Oswald Sanders, Enjoying Intimacy with God, 20.

3

LISTEN UP!

> *"The mark of a godly man and the mark of a godly church is that everything they do is God-initiated."*[1]
>
> *Manley Beasley*

West Point, our nation's primary military leadership academy, offers a study in seeming contradictions. Every year 4,000 cadets undergo rigorous training. It begins from day one with a rigid regimen to teach cadets how to live under authority. Their success in battle depends upon a willingness to follow commands without question, so their training in this is intense. But this training in rigid obedience is headed somewhere surprising: flexibility, the quality that enables them to adapt rapidly and effectively to changing battlefield conditions.

> *In the chaos of battle . . . leaders can't expect to stick to a fixed plan. They depend on the predictable competence of their subordinates (instilled by all of that training) as well as on their own judgment . . . "Everything that happens at West Point serves a question,"* says Ed Ruggero . . . "How do you develop an organization that can thrive amid constant change?"*[2]

For the military, detailed strategic plans are developed for the battles they may face. But the leaders must be keenly sensitive to the ever-changing conditions. They must maintain unbroken communication with the commander above them, then move without hesitation at his directives.

BATTLEFIELD READY

We often think of the church as a comfortable cruise ship. We board occasionally to get a few moments of relief and comfort, then go on about our life.

God sees it differently. He reminds us we are engaged in a cosmic battle for the lives of men. We do not wrestle against "flesh and blood, but against the rulers, against the powers, against the world forces of this darkness, against the spiritual forces of wickedness in the heavenly places" (Ephesians 6:12). If you've led for long in a local church that is seriously engaged in ministry, you quickly realize the magnitude of the forces against us. And you know the lives of people and the glory of God are at stake.

Our Commander knows we will not survive unless we put on the full armor of God and follow His lead. We must listen up, suit up, stand up, and pray up in the battle. And at every point, we must move forward with His plans, not ours.

The most important thing we must do is keep constant communication with the Commander-in-Chief. This is why Paul urges us, when suited in full armor, to pray "with all prayer and petition . . . at all times in the Spirit, and with this in view, be on the alert with all perseverance and petition for all the saints" (Ephesians 6:18).

There must be a consistency about our obedience and our unwavering submission to God's authority. God knows what He's doing. He sees the whole battle. When He says "move," we must obey. Our lives and those of others He loves are at stake. Like our ancient spiritual forefathers headed to the Promised Land, when God's pillar of fire moves we must follow, and when it stops we must not move ahead.

But this obedience requires great flexibility. When God's plan runs different to ours, we must gladly lay ours aside and go where He directs. Without this wonderful tension of strict obedience and surrendered flexibility, we will find ourselves wandering far from God's presence. And in a battlefield, filled with the land mines and schemes of the devil, that is deadly.

How do we maintain this spiritual tension and plan and move in ways that invite His presence? How do we accomplish the work of strategic planning, but do it under God's initiation?

UNDERSTAND GOD'S WAYS

Every person operates in certain habitual ways. "He always does that," someone might say about you. The problem is, many of our ways run counter to the desires of God.

God's ways are perfect. Although His ways are higher than our ways and His thoughts are higher than our thoughts, God has chosen to make many of His ways known to us (Isaiah 55:8–9). A Presence-Centered leader increasingly understands and cooperates with the ways of God that invite His presence.

One reason David was so effective as a leader was that he continually asked God to show him His ways so that he might cooperate more fully.

> *Make me know Your ways, O LORD;*
> *Teach me Your paths.*
> *Lead me in Your truth and teach me,*
> *For You are the God of my salvation;*
> *For You I wait all the day. (Psalm 25:4–5 emphasis added)*
>
> *Teach me Your way, O LORD,*
> *And lead me in a level path*
> *Because of my foes. (Psalm 27:11 emphasis added)*
>
> *I shall* **remember** *the deeds of the LORD;*
> *Surely I will* **remember** *Your wonders of old.*
> *I will* **meditate** *on all Your work*
> *And* **muse** *on Your deeds.*
> *Your way, O God, is holy;*
> *(Psalm 77:11–13 emphasis added)*
>
> *Teach me Your way, O LORD;*
> *I will walk in Your truth;*
> *Unite my heart to fear Your name.*
> *(Psalm 86:11 emphasis added)*

> *I will **meditate** on Your precepts*
> ***And regard** [look upon] **Your ways.***
> *(Psalm 119:15 emphasis added)*

David took the time to know God. He longed to discover God's standard operating procedures. In this study, David had one agenda: to walk in God's ways. He purposed to do nothing that would hinder God's presence, and everything that would invite it. And he wanted to lead others there also.

David knew that the path to this understanding was to look back with intensity. Notice the words of his prayers: "I will remember," "I will meditate," "I will muse on Your deeds," "I will regard Your ways." Can this be said of you? Do you take deliberate time in God's Word and study His activity in human history to see the patterns of God's behavior? If not, how do you expect to cooperate with Him? And as a leader, how can you take others there?

Tragically, it is possible to run counter to God's ways. To pay such little attention, we actually work against His presence. Job speaks of those who "do not even desire the knowledge of [God's] ways" (Job 21:14). All of us have been in church gatherings where God is nowhere to be found. People are singing, preaching, doing a great deal of religious activity, and feeling confident about their spiritual exercises. But God is not there. The worst indictment will come to leaders whose thinking is so misaligned that they are oblivious to the lack of God's presence.

God can do whatever He desires, whenever He desires, however He desires. But throughout history He has illustrated a pattern of His ways. Understanding these ways enlarges and directs our praying, living, and leading. It enables us, and those we lead, to respond more quickly. If we are oblivious to God's ways, we can miss His

> **If we are oblivious to God's ways, we can miss His activity.**

activity. But if we are wisely aware, we can cooperate more fully with His presence in each situation.

Particularly important in our day is to understand the ways of God in revival and spiritual awakening. In *OneCry: A Nationwide Call for Spiritual Awakening*, Byron Paulus and I define six revival realities.[3]

These are some of the evident, knowable ways of God when He seeks to revive His church and awaken the lost. God has repeated these ways countless times. So why would we not seek to understand this so we could better cooperate with God? Why would we not read and study everything we can to become the greatest authority in our city on the ways of God in revival in order to help others?

You can learn these ways of God and you must. Educate yourself and your people. The best tool for this learning, of course, is His Word.

If you desire to build a Presence-Centered church, study what invites God's presence and what aborts God's presence. Where does He seem to manifest Himself in human history? Where does He seem to manifest Himself in the church? What invites His presence? And when does He withdraw His presence—and why?

Isaiah gives us a powerful insight about what invites God's presence. He tells us to prepare a way for God and to remove all that would hinder His entrance. Then he reminds us of the two places God chooses to dwell.

> *And it will be said,*
> *"Build up, build up, prepare the way,*
> *Remove every obstacle out of the way of My people."*
> *For thus says the high and exalted One*
> *Who lives forever, whose name is Holy,*
> *"I dwell on a high and holy place,*
> *And also with the contrite and lowly of spirit*
> *In order to revive the spirit of the lowly*
> *And to revive the heart of the contrite."*
> *(Isaiah 57:14–15)*

If we long for the presence of Christ, we must not walk in pride. We must humble ourselves before the Lord. Humility means understanding who God is, who we are, and knowing the difference. The spirit that admits sin and acknowledges need, humility is always the first step to God's presence. Christ spoke of this poverty of spirit as the entry into His kingdom (Matthew 5:3). Only those who recognize their spiritual emptiness will hunger to experience God.

God dwells with people who are broken. These are not necessarily those who have been crushed by life's difficulties, but those who have surrendered their wills to the will of the Father. They have seen their desperate need of God so deeply that they are willing to be governed by another. This is God's way and it remains consistently true throughout the Scripture and human experience.

Along with studying Scripture, read great revival literature—especially the historical accounts of revival—for these revivals are the moments we see God in greater fullness. Ask God to open your eyes to His patterns. The Welsh Revival of 1904–1905 was preceded by several leaders and conventions that reminded the church of the ways of God in revival. By helping churches and leaders understand God's ways, this prepared the soil for the worldwide visitation that was about to occur.

The wonderful promise of Scripture is that God loves to cooperate with those who cooperate with Him. God "acts in behalf of the one who waits for Him," Isaiah said. "You meet him who rejoices in doing righteousness, who remembers You in Your ways" (Isaiah 64:4–5).

GOD-INITIATED PLANS

When Jesus was on earth, He always operated as a man. Though He was fully God, He laid aside those rights, privileges, and powers so He could be the perfect human sacrifice for our sins, and also model for us how a true man is to live.

Not only did He illustrate what we are to be and do, but He also showed us how we discover this moment by moment. How we are to function on this battlefield. How we listen and move at our Leader's commands.

Jesus' plan was simple: *He lived completely by God-initiation.*

> ***I can do nothing on My own initiative.*** *As I hear, I judge; and My judgment is just, because I do not seek My own will, but the will of Him who sent Me. (John 5:30 emphasis added)*

> *So Jesus said, "When you lift up the Son of Man, then you will know that I am He, **and I do nothing on My own initiative**, but I speak these things as the Father taught Me.*
>
> *"And He who sent Me is with Me; He has not left Me alone, for I always do the things that are pleasing to Him." As He spoke these things, many came to believe in Him. Jesus said to them, "If God were your Father, you would love Me, for I proceeded forth and have come from God, **for I have not even come on My own initiative,** but He sent Me." (John 8: 28–30, 42 emphasis added)*
>
> ***For I did not speak on My own initiative,** but the Father Himself who sent Me has given Me a commandment as to what to say and what to speak. (John 12:49 emphasis added)*
>
> *Do you not believe that I am in the Father, and the Father is in Me? The words that I say to you I do not **speak on My own initiative,** but the Father abiding in Me does His works. (John 14:10 emphasis added)*

Jesus spoke in these same terms about the Holy Spirit, who was to come at Pentecost to indwell all believers.

> *But when He, the Spirit of truth, comes, He will guide you into all the truth; for **He will not speak on His own initiative**, but whatever He hears, He will speak; and He will disclose to you what is to come. (John 16:13 emphasis added)*

If we want to lead our church to be saturated with the presence of God, we must make every decision and plan by God-initiation. Like the West Point cadets, we must keep the communication lines open ("pray without ceasing"), get our plans and direction from Him, then move instantly at His leading.

I have benefitted tremendously from men who have taught me how to do strategic planning (such as Bobb Biehl and his very helpful

Masterplanning process). Each year our elder and staff teams go through detailed planning. We use a system to evaluate where we have been, where we need to go, and what needs to happen for us to get there. This helps us see honestly and move intentionally. It keeps us from leadership laziness. But without the presence of Christ in that process, we are leading blind. We seek to move through that annual process with a keen sense of deep dependence upon God and His directing hand. Some of the questions we often ask ourselves are:

- *Is God in this?*
- *Do we sense His initiation?*
- *Have we prayed fully through this?*
- *Is this consistent with the revealed will of God in His Word? With God's ways?*
- *Is it violating some biblical directives?*
- *Is there unity among our leaders and a sense of God's clear direction?*
- *Do we lack peace or have hesitation in our hearts? If so, are we missing God or simply wavering with small faith?*
- *Is there recognizable spiritual energy as we dream of this plan?*
- *Do we find faith rising in our hearts to trust God for the extraordinary . . . the kinds of things He does when His presence is with us?*

God-initiated planning makes prayer much more than a perfunctory opening moment to our planning meetings. It demands that we be vitally connected to Him—individually and as a team. If we are to let God's presence guide the process, we must pray before we plan, as we plan, and after we plan.

SEIZING THE DIVINE MOMENT

There are also times when we have made a plan, even the right plan, but God has an unexpected turn for us—something we didn't see coming. His Spirit is moving, and He invites us to join Him. It may be outside our well-laid plans, even way beyond our comfort zone. It may be that God didn't reveal this earlier because we weren't ready for it yet. It almost always carries risk, for that is what faith is all about.

And it may run counter to our expectations of how God was going to work. If so, like West Point-trained leaders, we must move with flexibility. We must dial in carefully and make sure we are hearing the Commander, then trust His leadership and adapt.

When the mercy-drop of God's presence touched our church for a season in 2011, I was preaching a series on the Holy Spirit. On Sunday, April 3, I was dealing with a subject I had never taught in our church: the quenching of the Holy Spirit. Paul gives a clear command from God:

> *Do not quench the Spirit; do not despise prophetic*
> *utterances. But examine everything carefully; hold fast to*
> *that which is good; abstain from every form of evil.*
> *(1 Thessalonians 5:19–22)*

Like a fire that is burning brightly but is quenched with a bucket of water, we must not do anything that extinguishes God's movement. To understand this truth, we must look at the whole passage. "Do not despise prophetic utterances," Paul says. There are a wide variety of interpretations about what that means today. But at its minimum, everyone would agree it means something about the proclamation of God's truth to us by His Spirit and His Word. We are to listen carefully, examine to make sure it is accurate, then throw it out if it's not legitimate or move forward with it, if it is from God.

Let me illustrate.

A pastor has an unusual week in God's presence. As he studies the Word, he realizes that God wants to tell the people something deeply. Perhaps it's a call to prayer for the lost. He asks his wife and key leaders to pray, sensing that "God is up to something Sunday." He comes to the pulpit with spiritual anticipation and preaches his heart out. It is a great, hot message, straight from the heart of God.

People are deeply moved. Many come to him after the service, saying how it has affected them. Then they go to their cars and into their week—*and do not make one single spiritual adjustment to their lives!*

Instead, what would happen if God said to 200 people or 2,000, "Pray for the lost!" and they all prayed? Do you think God had some reason why He was calling His people (which He created and bought with His blood) to pray for the lost? Was He about to do something miraculous? About to manifest Himself in an extraordinary way through their prayers? To save many people? What could have happened?

But the people "quenched the Spirit." They doused the movement. God was moving, but their inflexibility and disobedience aborted the activity of God.

Often we are weak in following God's redirection. There are often times in a worship service when God begins to make Himself known. We all sense it. But we can run right past this moment and miss Him.

On Sunday, April 11, 2011, I was halfway through a message on this truth when the Lord told me to stop. The impression became overwhelming. And so I did—and told the people what I believed God was telling me to do.

Suddenly a retired missionary stood up and said, "We must obey God right now! We must not quench the Spirit any longer," then gave a tearful, impassioned plea. People immediately began to move to the altar. A lady came to share a testimony . . . and it soon formed into a waiting line. That service lasted until 3:00 in the afternoon. We came back the next night and the next—every night except Saturday for the next five weeks. This was one of the most glorious, spontaneous movements of God I've ever witnessed. The watchword of those days became, "Do not quench the Spirit."

We could have easily missed this divine moment. I could have been more interested in "my" sermon than God's leadership. I'm sure I've done that hundreds of times. The missionary could have feared "what people will think" and not exhorted us to obedience. The lady who came first to testify could have been fearful and never stepped from her seat. We could have never given people the opportunity to speak. I've been burned a few times when I've opened the microphone. Who hasn't? But the Lord was leading, and we needed to flex with His leadership.

If we want to be a church that is filled with the presence of God, we must let Him initiate our planning, but also let Him initiate unexpected turns that can be explained only in terms of His activity among us.

RE-ADJUSTMENTS
Only Jesus is infallible. Even the best of spiritual leaders can miss His initiation. I once asked one of my mentors, Manley Beasley, if he had ever missed God. He laughed as he told me he had missed God many

times. He also reminded me that each time you realize you've missed His voice is a wonderful learning moment. It equips you—if you pay attention—to hear better in the future.

Let's say we took 100 women, one of which was your mother, and put them on a parking lot. We blindfolded you and then asked each woman, one by one, to call out your name. When your mother called you would know it. Why? You had been with her. Years and years in her presence had given you the ability to know her voice.

The more we seek to move with God-initiation in our planning, the better we get. We discern His leadership more keenly. We find it easier to differentiate His voice from ours, the world's, or the devil's.

If we have missed Him (and we will many times), we need to humbly admit our failure, re-establish communication, and get back under His leadership.

A THREE-WORD EVALUATION

Great leaders and churches invite hard evaluation. They are humble enough to pull others into a room and appraise every activity. They ask tough questions and leave their egos at the door. Such times are not destructive discussions, but aggressive attempts to get better and better at what is done for God's kingdom.

If we want to move in God's presence, we should evaluate every worship service, small-group meeting, ministry function, and mission venture—every activity in our church—with a three-word question: *"Was God there?"* If God did not initiate what we did, we can be assured that He will not bless. He blesses His plans, not ours.

If God did not initiate it and He is not there, it is worse than destructive. We will misrepresent God. We will be telling people, "This is what an experience with God is like!" but it will be hollow.

If you long for His presence, let Him lead the planning . . . and let Him redirect the moments as He desires. He really is a good leader! Follow Him with instant obedience and spiritual flexibility.

1. Manley Beasley, as repeated to Bill Elliff many times.
2. http://www.fastcompany.com/42823/grassroots-leadership-us-military-academy
3. Byron Paulus and Bill Elliff, OneCry: A Nationwide Call for Spiritual Awakening, (Chicago: Moody Publishers, 2014).

4 ᘒ

REMOVE BARRIERS

> *"Mr. Gorbachev, tear down this wall!"*
>
> *President Ronald Reagan*
>
> *(Spoken before the Brandenburg gate in 1987 at the wall that had divided East and West Berlin for 26 years and been a symbol of Communist oppression. The gate was opened twenty-nine months later.)*

Bunker Buster bombs were created in World War II by British designer Barnes Wallis. They were designed to be dropped from almost four miles in the air, reaching velocities in excess of the speed of sound. These powerful bombs were developed not to penetrate the underground bunker, but to go through the earth beside it and create a mini-earthquake, exploding the bunker's foundation and creating a massive hole below the fortification. The stronghold would instantly collapse into the hole.

During the invasion of Iraq in Desert Storm, similar bombs were needed but none available. A stopgap measure was created in twenty-eight days with WWII bombs that were retro-fitted with laser-guidance. They were so effective that after a few weeks, all the Iraqi bunkers were destroyed, and the American forces marched in with little opposition.

THE CHURCH'S GREAT ENEMY
Satan is not ignorant. One of his greatest tactics is to develop spiritual and structural bunkers inside the church to oppose the movement of the Spirit of God. If unnoticed, these strongholds can become mighty

barriers to the activity and presence of God in the lives of His people. These bunkers are not hard to create, given the threefold attack by the world and its philosophies, the flesh and its weakness, and the devil and his schemes.

The rapid decline of many churches indicates these bunkers are present and well fortified. But they are no match for God's people when they follow His initiation in the power of His Spirit. Still, if we are interested in building a church where God's presence is manifested, we must not be naïve. We must accurately assess the true condition of our church. Sometimes, despite our best intentions, we will discover we are dealing with long-standing, deeply entrenched strongholds.

We must accurately assess the true condition of our church.

Once we detect them, we must rely on God's means to remove every barrier to His presence.

HEART BARRIERS

There are no sinless people or churches. Every Christian wrestles with temptation and failure. But often, sin in the lives of God's people has gone undetected or unchallenged—and created massive bunkers.

In the first church, Ananias and Sapphira were gripped by a materialism that caused them to deceive others and exaggerate their claims of giving. God was so concerned for His fledgling model, He used Peter to instantly identify and correct this hypocrisy. The result led to greater awe and surrender to Christ (Acts 5:1–11).

But in many churches, such sins have festered for years. The greatest loss is the absence of God's presence in the midst of His people. Sin is accepted and embraced. Strongholds develop. The result is a church with a shell of religion, but no reality.

My wife and I traveled for several years with Life Action Ministries. This wonderful ministry focuses on doing everything possible to help churches experience genuine revival.[1] We would bring a team to churches for two weeks to teach revival truths. Our first job was to find the bunkers. With experience, these are easy to detect.

Sometimes a church is filled with pride: pride in their history, their accomplishments, their buildings or programs, their music, even their tolerance of sin. The tragedy is that God opposes the proud. If we walk in pride we can expect, not His enabling grace, but His resistance (James 4:6). One great evidence of pride in a church or an individual is prayerlessness. If a church is weak in prayer, they believe they can do just fine without God.

When Christ addressed the churches in John's revelation He pointed out several bunkers. One church had lost its first love. They were doctrinally sound, but their passion for Christ was gone. Another was dreadfully lukewarm. Another filled with idolatry.

If Christ were to write a letter to your church, to what would He point? Is there:

- *Humility or pride?*
- *Generosity or materialism?*
- *Brokenness or stubbornness?*
- *Free-flowing forgiveness or judgmental unforgiveness?*
- *Holiness or immorality?*
- *Surrendered, willing service or selfishness?*
- *Authenticity and transparency or hypocrisy and covering?*
- *Edifying words or gossip and slander?*
- *Unconditional acceptance of others or proud prejudice?*
- *A burden for the lost or self-absorbed inwardness?*
- *Courage to follow Christ at any cost or fearfulness and timidity?*
- *A God-pleasing passion or a man-fearing spirit?*

The greatest question is: Do you know where the bunkers are? Have you taken the time to prayerfully evaluate your church—not in nit-picking, Pharisaic introspection—but with a genuine desire to see God's glory unleashed?

If you are oblivious to your church's true spiritual state, you will discover that the strongholds keep growing. I have noticed that many pastors discover these bunkers within the first eighteen months of their tenure. Often, they simply do not know what to do. Sometimes they fear taking the necessary steps and simply leave. This is one reason nine out of ten seminary graduates do not retire in vocational ministry. Many become so overwhelmed with the challenge of moving a church to health, they drop out of ministry. Sadly, other pastors are intimidated by the status quo and never address the issues that abort the presence of God.

If the spiritual leaders of a church—through ignorance, discouragement, or fear—do not address the real issues, these can become even more entrenched, making the next leader's task even greater. So what can we do?

Assess Accurately
Spend time asking God for His assessment of the spiritual condition of your church. Hear His answer on your knees. If there are spiritual bunkers, ask Him to open your eyes and others' eyes to see the real issues.

Gather key leaders to do honest assessment of the church's spiritual health. Pray through the next steps of addressing these issues. Take time to do some spiritual inventories. Each year we do a S.W.O.T. analysis. We gather the key leaders (at multiple levels) with a whiteboard and look honestly at the church's **S**trengths, **W**eaknesses, **O**pportunities (areas that could yield increased fruit) and **T**hreats (areas that could torpedo the ministry). Done with prayer and openness, this can be a church-changing exercise.

Bring in wise, godly leaders from the outside to help you see the real state of the church if needed. Humbly listen to their counsel. Often, fresh eyes can see what you cannot.

Pray Fervently
I once pastored a church that had some major bunkers. We tried everything to turn the ship, with little results. We became desperate and knew that only God could do what was necessary.

I invited all those willing to meet every morning at 6:30 a.m. to pray for forty days. A wonderful group of twenty-five to forty gathered daily. After several weeks, we entered into some of the most powerful praying I've ever experienced. God's presence was so thick, the forty days came and went and we continued that prayer meeting five days a week for eighteen months!

And God moved—not in the way I expected but in the way He had planned. The dramatic, powerful change was accomplished through the persevering prayers of God's people.

Preach with Truth and Grace

God says His word is like the hammer that shatters the rock (Jeremiah 23:29). The inspired writer of Hebrews described it like this:

> *For the word of God is living and active and sharper than any two-edged sword, and piercing as far as the division of soul and spirit, of both joints and marrow, and able to judge the thoughts and intentions of the heart. And there is no creature hidden from His sight, but all things are open and laid bare to the eyes of Him with whom we have to do.* (Hebrews 4:12–13)

We must trust God and His Word. Our job is not to convince and persuade, but to rightly divide the Word of truth. Lovingly but boldly proclaimed, it will cut through hearts like a sword and reveal what is soulish and carnal from what is spiritual. It will even reveal our thoughts, intentions, and motivations.

Never underestimate the power of persistent preaching filled with grace and truth. I can tell the spiritual condition of the churches I've pastored by reviewing the topics or books of the Bible the Lord led me to preach. God longs to speak to His people to help them grow to maturity and experience His presence. If you are a pastor, take your preaching seriously and approach it prayerfully. God knows what the people need. Let Him say what He desires. (More on this in Chapter 6.)

> Never underestimate the power of persistent preaching filled with grace and truth.

Disciple the Willing

Every church has people who long to experience God. Find these people and build around them. Help them grow. Give them opportunities for service and leadership. If you lack godly leaders, ask God to send some ready-made leaders to the church. Don't let evil, controlling men determine the church's destiny. Don't give so much attention to their brush-fires that it diverts you from discipling the leaders who will move the church forward.

Raise up a band of godly believers and watch them gradually move into rightful places of influence. Reach and disciple new people and let God's growth outweigh those unwilling to surrender to His control. Pay particular attention to developing the men of your church into godly, humble, Spirit-filled leaders.

Flood your small-group curriculum and every venue with materials that deal with the key heart issues. Do anything and everything to pour biblical truth into willing hearts.

Address the Issues
Sometimes, you must confront strongholds head-on. Every pastor has faced these battles. If we are not careful, we will find ourselves avoiding these conflicts. But if they come, realize God is at work. He is performing the essential tasks to blast away whatever is aborting His presence and power in the church. It is hard work, but necessary. Don't run and don't quit. These are the seasons that need prayerful, persevering leadership. What are we doing as spiritual leaders if we don't give our all to see the church's heart brought to full surrender?

If you are tempted to give up, encourage yourself with this question: What is more important than God's presence? It is worth every sacrifice to open a highway for God?

Also be encouraged by this reality: We have mighty weapons to pull down barriers. We may not be using them, but they are available. The apostle Paul modeled this for us:

> *For though I do still live the life of a physical human creature, I am not waging this war in accordance with physical human standards, for the weapons used in my warfare are not mere human ones, but through my God are mighty for demolishing fortresses. For I am demolishing arguments and every barrier that is raised against the genuine knowledge of God. (2 Corinthians 10:3–5 WILLIAMS)*

It's a noble task to seek to redeem a church for whom Christ died—worth our very lives. So don't give up. Get counsel from seasoned pastors who have engaged in similar battles.

I've written a book specifically addressing these issues, drawing from my experiences and those of others. If you face tough issues, you may be helped by reading *Whitewater: Navigating the Rapids of Church Conflict.*[2]

STRUCTURAL BARRIERS

Sometimes the barriers that obstruct the flow of God's presence are issues of structure and methodology.

I consulted for a church that had dwindled to a third of its previous size. Once vibrant, it had lost its way. Though the pastor had left, a leadership team of eight strong men longed to see their church revived. They asked me to come help them.

In one retreat session, I realized part of the problem were the wineskins of the church. (Wineskins are simply the things churches develop to hold and release the life of Christ. Wineskins could be programs, ministries, personnel, systems, buildings, and structure: the way the church does things.) I asked them to list all their ministries. At the time, the church had approximately 300 people attending. Half were adults, with a core of about seventy-five people serving in volunteer positions.

To their amazement, they discovered they were trying to maintain more than sixty active ministries! Most were relics that had long since outlived their usefulness. Their wineskins weren't working. The people were worn out and the ministries were ineffective.

Tragically, their busyness made no room for the church's most essential work. They were not using God's means of grace to open the door for the presence of Christ.

Jesus had a strong, prophetic word about this.

> *And no one puts new wine into old wineskins; otherwise the new wine will burst the skins and it will be spilled out, and the skins will be ruined. But new wine must be put into fresh wineskins. (Luke 5:37–38)*

Every church needs new wine (the presence of Christ) and new wineskins (ways to hold and release the wine). If you have wineskins without wine, it's simply a shell. If you have new wine without proper wineskins, a rupture will occur.

The people Jesus was addressing understood this picture. Everyone in Jesus' day knew that once grapes had been crushed, the juice was placed in fresh wineskins for aging and eventual use. They knew wineskins must be:

Flexible

New wine must be put into new wineskins to allow for fermenting and expansion. If the skins are not supple, they will burst, wasting both the wineskin and the wine.

Jesus is telling us the wineskins used in a church must be able to adapt, to move to allow for growth. In the New Testament, God seldom defines the wineskins of the church. He simply illustrates the church's purposes (worship, community, spiritual growth, ministry, missions, stewardship) and the means of grace He prescribes (preaching, baptism, the Lord's Supper, prayer, giving, discipling, etc.). But He gives few instructions about the forms or methods to carry out these purposes. This indicates His desire for adaptability in methods so His purposes can be accomplished in different times and cultures.

One core value of a church should be a willingness to change—to adapt, to be flexible, to be open to the Spirit's initiation about any program or ministry. Sometimes this means deleting a ministry that has outlived its effectiveness or beginning something new. Wineskins are not sacred. Wine is.

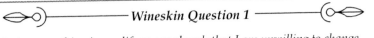

Is there anything in my life or our church that I am unwilling to change so that Christ's presence may be experienced more fully?

Functional

There is only one purpose for a wineskin: to hold and release the wine! It's simply a tool. This is how we must see every system and ministry in our church. Every year, evaluate every wineskin's effectiveness and value. Is it still accomplishing its purpose? Are there better ways to do that? Any wise vineyard owner regularly checks his wineskins, then replaces or repairs any ineffective ones. He understands the value of the wine.

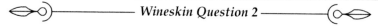

Are all our wineskins effective? Are they doing what God intended when they were first developed?

Filled

Wineskins are worthless until filled. In Jesus' day they were usually created from a goatskin. What a sad waste for a goat to give his life for his skin to be placed on a shelf and never filled with wine!

A church program or ministry is designed to be filled with the life of God. Without God's presence and power, it's worse than useless because it diverts time, energy, and focus from what really matters. It could be that God has no interest in inhabiting that wineskin. Or something could be hindering God's presence in a potentially good ministry.

Is each of our current wineskins filled with the life of God? Is the wineskin itself aborting God's presence or is something wrong with it that prevents the presence of Christ? What change is needed?

Flowing

Imagine this scene. A farmer has gone to incredible lengths to plow the ground, plant grape vines, then water, fertilize, and wait several years for the vines to produce. He tends the vines to maximize the harvest. When the grapes are harvested, he takes them to the facility he has built. Through a series of vats and sieves, he crushes and purifies the wine.

At the same time, he has raised and butchered some goats to create fresh wineskins (no easy process, especially for the goat!). He takes the new wine, pours it in the fresh wineskins, then sits back to enjoy what he has produced.

A weary traveler comes to his door and asks, "Do you have anything to drink?"

"Yes," says the farmer. "I have many wonderful goatskins filled with wine. They are laid up in my barn. Come and see!"

The traveler eyes the array of full wineskins. "May I have a drink?"

"Oh, no!" says the famer. "I produced those so I could keep them in my barn. Every day I go out and look at them. I have more wineskins than any of my neighbors. I have the best wine and wineskins in the country. But I don't plan to drink the wine."

In Jesus' day, wine was produced to quench the thirst of the weary. The entire purpose of a wineskin was to hold and release its wine.

Many churches love to sit and enjoy their wineskins. They have created bigger and better programs, buildings, and resources. They take pride in what they've developed. But who is receiving the wine? Is the life of God flowing through those containers to help weary people? If not, something is dreadfully wrong.

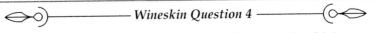

Wineskin Question 4

Is the life of Christ flowing through the wineskins of our church? Are people inside and outside the church encountering the presence of Christ? Do we see lives changed by the power of God?

Assessment is hard; change is even harder. But we must deal, in God's time and way, with the barriers that abort His presence. If you are tempted to ignore the truths of this chapter, ask yourself two questions:

What good is a church that isn't filled and flowing with the presence of Christ?

What will you do about it?

1. To learn more about Life Action, go to www.LifeAction.org.
2. Bill Elliff, Whitewater: Navigating the Rapids of Church Conflict (Little Rock, AR.: TruthInk Publications, 2009).

5

CREATE ENVIRONMENTS

> *"The patriarch Jacob . . . saw a vision of God and cried out
> in wonder, 'Surely the Lord is in this place; and I knew it
> not . . .' That was his trouble, and it is ours."*[1]
>
> A. W. Tozer

"Every pastor needs a good garden," said the well-meaning deacon in
one of my early churches. I was hard-pressed to make the connection
between pastoring and farm labor. But since the parsonage had a huge
backyard and I was intrigued by the thought of a bountiful harvest, and
chiefly since the deacon said he'd plow and plant the garden, I agreed.
What I didn't know is that gardens don't come with an instruction
manual. And gardening is hard work.

I was busy with my wife and two little children, as well as pastoring
my first church after seminary. I kept thinking, I need to water that
garden, but I couldn't find the time. The Oklahoma sun beat down, and
the continual wind quickly dried the seedlings. And somehow I didn't
realize a garden needed daily weeding.

What the garden needed most was the presence of a good gardener!
Every day I should have been in the midst of those plants, hoeing the
weeds and tending the shoots. I could maintain a healthy environment
for growth only through my continual presence and care.

This became woefully evident at the end of the season. I'm ashamed to
admit I harvested from my massive, weed-filled garden only one ear
of corn!

CHRIST'S CONCENTRIC CIRCLES

What does it take for a child, a student, a young couple, a single adult, or a married adult to grow spiritually? To develop into a fully devoted, fruitful and productive follower of Jesus Christ?

A church can't make people grow. But it can, by the grace and direction of God, create environments where growth is possible when tended by the Master Gardener. No one illustrated this more clearly than Christ as He lived on earth as a man.

Of all the things that could have been written about Christ's pre-teen years, there is only one small story. It is recorded for us when Jesus left his family caravan on the way home from Jerusalem. Jesus, unknown to His family, remained in the temple in Jerusalem. His family left to go home and realized that Jesus was not with them.

> *Then, after three days they found Him in the temple, sitting in the midst of the teachers, both listening to them and asking them questions. And all who heard Him were amazed at His understanding and His answers.*
>
> *When they saw Him, they were astonished; and His mother said to Him, "Son, why have You treated us this way? Behold, Your father and I have been anxiously looking for You."*
>
> *And He said to them, "Why is it that you were looking for Me? Did you not know that I had to be in My Father's house?"*
>
> *But they did not understand the statement which He had made to them.*
>
> *And He went down with them and came to Nazareth, and He continued in subjection to them; and His mother treasured all these things in her heart.*
>
> *And Jesus kept increasing in wisdom and stature, and in favor with God and men. (Luke 2:46–52)*

Jesus grew. And He kept growing, as a human in perfect union with His Father, all the way to His death. In this early scene we see Him lingering in His "Father's house." The presence of God represented by the temple in Jerusalem was an important environment for growth. Then we see him as a young boy, "continuing in subjection" to his parents—another ideal environment for this growing boy.

> **If these concentric relational circles were important for Christ, shouldn't they be even more important for us?**

As we observe the three years of His public ministry, we see Jesus deliberately place Himself in various relational environments. I'm not speaking of geographic locations, but people groups. Each, it seems, was essential for His life and growth—and the growth of those around Him. If these concentric relational circles were important for Christ, shouldn't they be even more important for us?

We cannot make people in the church grow. But we can develop the right environments where growth is possible through people's encounters with Christ and others.

One-to-One

Everything in Jesus' life centered in personal intimacy with His Father. Jesus was always in communion with God. He modeled for us prayer without ceasing. He told His disciples that He did only what He saw His Father doing and said what He heard the Father saying (John 8:28–30). The Scriptures record multiple times when He went off to spend extended times with His Father.

> *In the early morning, while it was still dark, Jesus got up, left the house, and went away to a secluded place, and was praying there. (Mark 1:35)*
>
> *It was at this time that He went off to the mountain to pray, and He spent the whole night in prayer to God. (Luke 6:12)*
>
> *And He came out and proceeded as was His custom to the Mount of Olives; and the disciples also followed Him . . .*

> *and He withdrew from them about a stone's throw, and He knelt down and began to pray. (Luke 22:39–41)*

If we long to be a Presence-Centered church, we must make this our first priority. We as leaders must live in intimacy with the Father, then do whatever necessary to lead our people to see this as their greatest need and highest privilege.

How could we possibly lead a church if we are not in constant communion with Him? How can we find the needed direction without His guidance? Do we really believe it's possible to win the battle over "principalities and powers and world forces of this present darkness" if we will not "pray at all times in the Spirit, and with this in view, be on the alert with all perseverance and petition for all the saints" (Ephesians 6:12–19)?

We can't expect to be a church where God is pleased to dwell unless we daily, constantly turn our attention to the Father through His Word, prayer, and humble dependence. As pastors, we must teach our leaders and people that this is the foundational environment for them to meet God every day. We need to devote much time and attention to train our people how to encounter God on their own.

One of the easiest ways to begin this is to teach people how to read the Bible. Just read it. Over and over. Systematically. Ever year. Give them instructions. Share plans. Teach them the simple process of SOAP, which is Scripture, Observations, Applications, and Prayer. Because it is so important, our church devotes the first Sunday of every year to encouraging our people to read the Scripture. Teach people how to journal. Do anything and everything to teach and encourage people into the presence of God.

It starts here.

The Inner Three

Although Jesus was often around crowds, there is another relational environment He knew was essential. Jesus spent a great deal of time with two to three men who were closest to him: Peter, James, and John. In retrospect, we know they were to become the pillars of the early church and they needed the closer intimacy of this training with Christ.

Certainly there was something in each of them that was uniquely needed for the movement ahead. Maybe there was even something that Christ, as a man, needed from these men and the close, loving, discipling relationship they enjoyed. There was certainly much they gained from intimacy with each other.

Everybody needs a mentor, and everyone needs to be mentoring or discipling others. We need close friendships. We need people who will love and accept us just as we are, but challenge us to be more. The apostle Paul also modeled this, always traveling with a small group. But within that group we see him linked with key men: Paul and Barnabas, Paul and Timothy.

If you want to develop a church where the presence of God is evident, help people connect in small, accountability friendships with one to two others, men with men and women with women. People encounter God in these relationships in ways that do not occur anywhere else.

Small Groups

The most easily identifiable group in Christ's life was the Twelve. The main thing we see him doing is discipling these men. Why just twelve? Numerous studies have shown that twelve people is the optimum size for a small group. What a coincidence!

Jesus taught these men, ate with these men, retreated with these men. They did life together. One of the greatest verses on discipleship is recorded the day Christ pulled these twelve into a group.

> *And He appointed twelve, so that they would **be with Him** and that He could send them out to preach, and to have authority to cast out the demons. (Mark 3:14–15 emphasis added)*

His manner of developing these men was simple: He was filled with God, and they would "be with Him." Period. This unique method ensured they felt and saw the presence of Christ in every experience of the common day. They saw how Jesus dealt with His opponents and His friends, how He paid His taxes, how He ate, how He slept (even in the middle of a storm). We may wonder why it took only three years to train men to change the world, but the training was 24/7.

This environment had a great purpose: to equip them to spread the gospel ("send them out to preach") and overcome the spiritual enemies of this world ("have authority to cast out the demons").

A Presence-Centered church must grow smaller even as it grows larger. Every person should be a part of a small group. This should be more than a one-hour Bible study. It must be the joining of lives: eating, serving, laughing, crying, and experiencing God together. You need what others bring to a small group, and they need your unique gifts and contribution to their lives.

The constant evaluation for a small group leader is not: "Did that Bible study go well?" Instead, leaders should ask:

- *"Was God here?"*
- *"Did we encounter Him?"*
- *"Are lives being changed because we have invited His presence into this environment?"*
- *"Are the people in our group being equipped to share the gospel and stand against the Enemy's attacks because Christ's presence has been experienced?"*

The Core

Inside each church is a core of people who are all-in. It may be 10 people, 200, or 2,000, but these are the deeply committed laborers who can say with Paul, "For me, to live is Christ!" (Philippians 1:21). For these folks, the kingdom of God and its advancement is why they exist. To them the church is not peripheral, but central. They are generally the ones who give, serve, pray, and lead.

Jesus had a group of seventy who fit this description.

> *Now after this the Lord appointed seventy others, and sent them in pairs ahead of Him to every city and place where He Himself was going to come.*
>
> *And He was saying to them, "The harvest is plentiful, but the laborers are few; therefore beseech the Lord of the harvest to send out laborers into His harvest. "Go; behold, I send you out as lambs in the midst of wolves . . .*
>
> *"Whatever city you enter and they receive you, eat what is set before you; and heal those in it who are sick, and say to them, 'The kingdom of God has come near to you.'"*
> *(Luke 10:1–9)*

These disciples returned to the Lord with joy, awed that even the demons of hell were subject to them. Their courageous service caused Jesus to "rejoice greatly" (Luke 10:21). It thrilled His heart to see His core team experience the power of God in ministry. Little did they realize the preparation that was occurring for what lay ahead in launching the church.

I remember vividly one of the first worship services where I was asked to preach. I was 17 and scared to death. A dear friend of my father's had taken a risk to let me preach in his church on a Sunday night. I had prepared with my father's help a sermon I prayed would last more than ten minutes! But I couldn't seem to overcome my fear.

The evening I was to preach, my daily devotional reading was in Jeremiah, Chapter 1, and the words leaped off the page to my heart.

> *Now the word of the LORD came to me saying, "Before I formed you in the womb I knew you, and before you were born I consecrated you; I have appointed you a prophet to the nations."*
>
> *Then I said, "Alas, Lord GOD! Behold, I do not know how to speak, because I am a youth."*
>
> *But the LORD said to me, "Do not say, 'I am a youth,' because everywhere I send you, you shall go, and all that I command you, you shall speak. Do not be afraid of them, for I am with you to deliver you," declares the LORD.*
>
> *Then the LORD stretched out His hand and touched my mouth, and the LORD said to me, "Behold, I have put My words in your mouth." (Jeremiah 1:4–9)*

I have never recovered from that moment as I experienced God speaking to me, then through me. Something about being thrust into ministry forces you to cry out for God's presence. When He manifests Himself in ministry, you are never the same.

Can you imagine the thrill these seventy disciples felt when Christ acknowledged them, commissioned them, and entrusted ministry to them? Authentic followers of Christ want to be used. When spiritual leaders train and release others in ministry, these new servants must find God.

> Something about being thrust into ministry forces you to cry out for God's presence.

As they experience Christ's presence in fresh ways, they realize even more that this is their destiny. They learn at a more rapid pace. They grow more quickly. They experience the ecstasy and agony of ministering to others. And God uses them to bring His presence and power to needy people. There's nothing more empowering.

Many churches lack an intentional path to develop their core for service and ministry. They fail to provide this environment for their people. If you want your key people to go deeper into God's presence, find a way to equip them and engage them in ministry. People grow more quickly if they serve.

As appropriate, gradually give them more authority in leadership. This ensures you won't be building adolescents who never grow to adulthood. Model shared leadership. Give it away. God always has more.

If you seek to build a church where God is present and "rejoicing greatly," then find and develop the core and send them out. Watch hell fall and heaven rejoice.

The Congregation

Jesus also engaged with what we could call the congregation. The 500 and the 5,000-plus were gathered in large groups to sit at Christ's feet and learn from Him. The crowd was a mixture of believers and unbelievers, but all were confronted with the living Christ.

Can you imagine the power of these moments as the Son of God opened their eyes to the truth of Scripture? When He told them what the kingdom of God was all about and invited them to follow Him there? What it must have felt like to look around and realize there were thousands listening, a great movement was happening, and they were invited to take part! Imagine what they experienced as they sat and worshiped in the literal presence of Christ.

Jesus was modeling that there is something powerful about a large gathering when He is present. After His ascension, the early church confirmed this. The church in Jerusalem regularly met in Solomon's Portico (an area on the Temple Mount that could hold thousands) and from "house to house" in smaller groups. Each played a vital role in the church's spontaneous expansion.

Some feel that this larger, congregational environment is not necessary in our present day, but the testimony of Scripture would disagree.

During times of persecution in church history, the only means for believers to gather has been in small groups, usually in homes. But when religious freedom is realized, the first response of the church is to gather everyone together. It's been happening for 2,000 years.

God has designed us to need both. A simple reading of the historical beginnings of the church illustrates this wonderful balance.

> *And all those who had believed were together (Acts 2:44)*
>
> *Day by day continuing with one mind in the temple, and breaking bread from house to house (Acts 2:46)*
>
> *Go, stand and speak to the people in the temple the whole message of this Life. (Acts 5:20)*
>
> *And every day, in the temple and from house to house, they kept right on teaching and preaching Jesus as the Christ. (Acts 5:42)*
>
> *So the twelve summoned the congregation of the disciples (Acts 6:2)*
>
> *When they had arrived and gathered the church together (Acts14:27)*
>
> *The apostles and the elders came together to look into this matter . . . All the people kept silent, and they were listening to Barnabas and Paul . . . Then it seemed good to the apostles and the elders, with the whole church . . . So when they were sent away, they went down to Antioch; and having gathered the congregation together, they delivered the letter. (Acts 15:6, 12, 22, 30)*
>
> *When he had landed at Caesarea, he went up and greeted the church (Acts 18:22)*
>
> *He withdrew from them and took away the disciples, reasoning daily in the school of Tyrannus. (Acts 19:9)*
>
> *On the first day of the week, when we were gathered together to break bread, Paul began talking to them,*

intending to leave the next day, and he prolonged his
message until midnight. (Acts 20:7)

While not every passage indicates the church's geographic location in a large setting, most of them do. And all of them indicate that there was some means of establishing the corporate identity of the whole. Notice, also, the purposes that were accomplished by the large-group gatherings. (*See Appendix D for a brief comparison of the value of large and small groups.*)

The ultimate example of the church is seen in heaven. The Revelation of John contains accounts of myriads of people gathered for corporate worship and communication. Large, glorious gatherings of worship. This is the church as it should and ultimately will be. The earthly church is meant to be a prototype of this eternal church.

If this is what God plans in fullness for heaven, then we should experience this on earth as much as possible. We must value small groups, but also large groups where vision is cast and people feel they are involved in a great movement.

How can we cooperate with God in developing congregational environments blessed by His presence? Because of its importance, the following chapter will explore that topic.

ONE FINAL NOTE

Just as Christ drew away and spent whole nights in prayer, we need not only the routine environments of God's presence, but also deliberate, concentrated seasons as a church to seek the Lord. Christ had ready access to the Father, but He began His ministry with forty days of fasting and prayer. Paul preceded his ministry by spending three years of solitude and preparation in the desert.

Churches need resolute, extended seasons seeking God's presence. Times where everything is set aside to "seek the Lord while He may be found; call upon Him while He is near" (Isaiah 55:6). Wise leaders will cooperate with God in creating such times of intense searching or intense service. Both are needed.

We must create multiple environments, as Jesus did, for people to experience the varied opportunities for God's presence. A great model for our churches is to develop our ministries around these concentric circles, making sure that all are available—and all are saturated with the life of God.

I had the privilege to grow up in a wonderful home. My grandfather and father were both godly men and pastors. Their wives were precious, praying helpmeets. I had my moments of struggle and rebellion, but the environments I experienced left me a legacy for which I am ever grateful. Some were planned and routine. Some were special and never to be repeated. Some were with single members of my family. Others with the whole group. All these environments helped me grow. But the most valuable component of my home life? God was there in each setting; that made all the difference.

The church family is called to create multiple, healthy environments—all filled with God's presence—where growth occurs and the kingdom expands.

1. A.W. Tozer, The Pursuit of God, (Camp Hill, Penn.: Christian Publications, 1982).

6

EXPERIENCE DEEPLY

> "At the heart of the Christian message is God Himself
> waiting for His redeemed children to push in to conscious
> awareness of His Presence. That type of Christianity
> which happens now to be the vogue knows this Presence
> only in theory. It fails to stress the Christian's privilege of
> present realization . . . The fiery urge that drove men like
> McCheyne is wholly missing. And the present generation of
> Christians measures itself by this imperfect rule."[1]
>
> A. W. Tozer

"Are you hungry?" said the country cook to the stranger who walked into her diner. Delightful smells from the kitchen filled the building.

"Famished."

"You've come to the right place," she said. "How about startin' off with some homemade biscuits? Nothin' store-bought here!"

"Would there be some butter and honey to go with those?"

"Absolutely," she said. "Cream gravy if you'd like. And alongside of that, any vegetable you'd want. I've got it all back in the kitchen."

He swallowed hard. "I can't believe it! I've come to diner heaven!"

"But the best thing is my fried chicken. Golden brown and just the right moisture inside," she said with a smile. "And if you're good, I've got homemade peach cobbler with a scoop of ice cream for dessert!"

The weary traveler was beside himself. He asked about the details of every item on her menu.

She was proud to rehearse the wonders she'd created. Obviously knowledgeable about country cooking, this was one customer she was excited to feed.

"I'm so glad you've cooked all this food," he said. "That was a wonderful explanation of your menu. It's exactly what I need and want!" Then he tipped his hat and walked out the door.

Seeming interest, good explanation, obvious need, but it resulted in no experience. A picture of the Sunday morning response of millions of American Christians.

> **ex-pe-ri-ence:** the fact or state of having been affected by or gained knowledge through direct observation or participation.[2]

Imagine talking about a great zoo or museum, but never walking through its wonders. Discussing the taste of a delicious meal, but never eating. Writing about the joys of marriage, but never taking the leap. Studying airplanes until you're an armchair expert, but never taking a flight. Explaining God, but never experiencing Him?

What good is almost anything if not experienced?

THE EXPERIENCE ABOVE

To understand how to experience God in worship, we need to begin by looking up. Heaven is not merely a future hope, but a present model. Walk with me, in your mind's eye, into heaven.

In heaven, everyone experiences God . . . all the time! There is no sin to distract. No world, flesh, or devil to pull you away. In glory there are no idle onlookers. No theologians merely talking about God but not enjoying Him. No back-row pew sitters tipping their hat weekly and living the rest of the week as if God didn't exist. No businessman idling in the foyer, checking his watch so he can get through with heaven's worship and go do something "really important." Everyone in heaven experiences God and His glory fully and continually. This is what God intended—the way life was created to be. That's why it's called heaven!

Jesus commanded us to pray fervently that God's kingdom would come and His will be done on earth as it is in heaven (Matthew 6:10). We are to look into the heavenlies and, in cooperation with our revealing God, pray that reality down to our daily experience. He wouldn't command us to pray this if it weren't possible.

Part of that prayer and search should be that we pursue the experiences of heaven as His body when we gather together. That, by God's grace, we would experience overwhelming love, continual peace, ecstatic joy, the satisfaction of service, the beauty of holiness, the amazement of God's creativity, and the thrill of His presence—the glory of God!

If you want a goal for your weekly gatherings as a church, there it is! Pray for the experiences of heaven. Prayerfully join with God in planning what He desires each time you gather. Resist the mindless droning of songs and messages not sent from above. Make sure, the best you can, that you lead people to encounter God, for that is the foundation and fullness of heaven and our greatest goal on earth.

> **If you want a goal for your weekly gatherings as a church, there it is! Pray for the experiences of heaven.**

LIMITED, BUT NOT LOST

Although we are limited by the confines of this present darkness, God longs for us to experience heavenly worship. We must grow in our understanding of how this occurs—and our part in the process. But the Lord of glory is eager for us to encounter Him in greater measures, for He knows the satisfaction we receive will make the world's gods seem worthless. And He realizes that the most fiery, unstoppable witnesses for Him are those who have walked with Him until they've cried, "Were not our hearts burning within us while He was speaking to us . . .?" (Luke 24:32).

> *God is so vastly wonderful, so utterly and completely delightful that he can, without anything other than Himself, meet and overflow the deepest demands of our total nature, mysterious and deep as that nature is. Such worship . . . can never come from a mere doctrinal knowledge of God. Hearts that are "fit to break" with love for the Godhead are those who have been in the Presence*

God is repulsed by empty performances, no
matter how professional. He is not moved to
display Himself when He is not consulted.
He is not impressed with man-initiated
programming. He leaves the gathering when
some proud, silly human seeks to build a
reputation. Jesus knows that what His children
need is not the façade of worship, but the
substance. Not a menu, but a meal. Not a
mere explanation of something that might be
available someday, but increasing experiences
of His reality now.

> Jesus knows
> that what
> His children
> need is not
> the façade of
> worship, but
> the substance.
> Not a menu,
> but a meal.

Most of all, He deserves the love, honor, attention, adoration, and
dominion that will spring only from experiences in His presence. He's
receiving such affection in heaven, but He deserves it every day from us
on earth.

So how can cooperate with Him so we leave our gatherings singing,
"Heaven came down and glory filled my soul!"?

ENTER HIS GATES WITH SINGING

If you want good advice, ask an expert. In this department a wise choice
is David, the man after God's own heart, the sweet psalmist of Israel.

> *Shout joyfully to the LORD, all the earth.*
> *Serve the LORD with gladness;*
> *Come before Him with joyful singing.*
> *Know that the LORD Himself is God;*
> *It is He who has made us, and not we ourselves;*
> *We are His people and the sheep of His pasture.*
> *Enter His gates with thanksgiving*
> *And His courts with praise.*
> *Give thanks to Him, bless His name.*
> *For the LORD is good;*
> *His lovingkindness is everlasting*
> *And His faithfulness to all generations. (Psalm 100)*

Here is a worshiper who knows how to enter God's presence and take others with him. Notice the verbs he uses to call us to worship: shout, serve, come, know, enter, give. Does this describe your experience? Shouldn't we evaluate our worship with these words?

- *Are we shouting to the Lord?*
- *Serving Him (not ourselves) with gladness?*
- *Coming before Him (not merely before others to impress them) with joyful singing?*
- *Taking time to meditate and remember that the Lord, He is God? That we are not God, but He is, and bowing before Him in humility?*
- *Are we remembering that He is the One who made us, and not we ourselves? That we are His people and the sheep of His pasture? That everything we are and have comes from Him?*
- *Are we constantly entering His gates with thanksgiving? Not grumbling, complaining, or whining?*
- *Are we entering His courts with praise? Does it take thirty minutes for us to approach praise or are we prepared and entering with praise?*
- *Are we giving to the Lord, not just receiving? Are we coming to God's presence just to get something and evaluating that time in light of how it pleased us, not Him? Are we giving our thanks, our worship, our attention, our time, our surrender? Is there anything we are unwilling to give Him?*
- *And are we basing our worship on the understanding that He is good, loving, kind, and forever faithful? Or do we come doubting God's goodness and faithfulness?*

Wouldn't it be like heaven if we entered our gatherings of worship like this? If we gave Him these affections and actions of worship, wouldn't God be pleased to dwell with us?

And wouldn't it be life changing if the people of your church knew how to live like this all the time? For worshiping God is not meant to be merely the goal of an hour on Sunday, but the experience of every moment of every day.

Learn the Art

We don't automatically know how to worship in these ways. For years, we have been conditioned otherwise. We are masters at worshiping ourselves. We can easily fill a room with noise. We are skilled at ignoring

God. But worshiping Him in spirit and truth represents a 180-degree turn from our humanistic lives. It is a learned art.

> *To great sections of the Church the art of worship has been lost entirely, and in its place has come that strange and foreign thing called the "program."*[4]

In worship, like every other area of life, we need the renewing of our minds that will transform our lives (Romans 12:2). We should let God teach us heavenly worship through His Word, by His Spirit. We must learn how to meditate on Him in private, studying His Word, listening to His Spirit, communing in prayer. Public worship must be an overflow of private worship.

And we must help our people. We should teach and preach on true worship. If we sense a distracted congregation, we should stop and exhort them, not with a mere, "Hey, everybody sing loud now," but with insight from God's Word that explains what real worship is, why it is so valuable, how we accomplish it, and why God deserves such praise.

We should teach our people to prepare for worship: how to "enter in." Most of our worship is wasted on ears that are full of the week's noise and minds crammed with the world's agenda. We may need to begin by calling our people to worship.

If you are a leader in worship (and you are, whether it's in your home, with those you disciple, in your small group, or before thousands—and it has very little to do with singing) it's your responsibility to seek Him until you find Him and begin to hear the songs of heaven. Only then can you lead others there. Learn the art.

Plan Prayerfully
There's nothing wrong with planning for worship. Look at the intricacies of the temple worship in the Old Testament (another prototype of heaven) and see the seriousness, the deliberation, the exactness with which the Levites prepared.

But there is everything wrong with manipulative planning—planning that begins with the wrong motivation, simply to elicit a desired response, but not from the glow of God's presence.

Emotions are deeply involved in worship. Do you love your spouse or children with no emotion? If so, something's wrong. But seeking to produce affections without awareness of God—His goodness, His power, His beauty—is merely manipulation. That won't impress a watching Sovereign.

Real worship is based on seeing and knowing Him. Remember that the truth of our songs, hymns, and spiritual songs—not merely the beat, the drive, the emotion—should move us to "Know that the LORD Himself is God; it is He who has made us, and not we ourselves" (Psalm 100:3). Experiential truth is what stirs our hearts in praise.

We will never hear heaven if we begin with prayerless planning. Our planning, first and foremost, should be listening. We should think deeply and prayerfully before the Lord about what He wants to say, where He wants to go in our gatherings. How foolish to think this could happen in a few minutes on the run. When we approach planning prayerlessly, we deprive our people, deceive ourselves, and perhaps even abort the manifest presence of God Himself.

We will never hear heaven if we begin with prayerless planning.

And, it's unlikely that God-planned worship would move randomly from one topic to another. God is always seeking to say something to us and give us the opportunity to express something to Him. So it would seem there would be a cohesion, an almost effortless flow to worship that comes from heaven. Not a forced theme, but God speaking on what He desires. It takes time to hear this and a lifetime to learn this. But it is not wasted effort, for all our labor and experiences are preparation for the business of eternity.

Selah Quietly

We have lost the art of the pause. The "Selah" at the end of multiple songs from the psalmist means to "pause and meditate" on what's been said or sung. Many worshipers aren't comfortable with silence. But often in the silence we can best hear the "still, small voice" for which our soul searches.

If you sense God speaking, give room for His voice. What He has to say to His people—individual-by-individual—is more important than anything we can say. Don't be afraid of the silence, for He commands, "Be still, and know that I am God" (Psalm 46:10 KJV).

Shift Gladly

We don't always plan it perfectly. Often the Lord loves to surprise us in worship, just to remind us He is in charge! A tenacious grasp on our "order of worship" can be deadly. Before every gathering, lay your plans at His feet. Remind yourself that He is the Leader of this moment and good at what He does. Give Him the freedom to go wherever He desires and change whatever He wants. Welcome His glorious interruptions. You will find they bring the sweetest, most powerful experiences.

CUT IT STRAIGHT IN THE POWER OF THE SPIRIT

God has ordained preaching as a primary way we encounter Him. A crucial part of our gathered worship through which we receive His enabling grace. So we must be careful that our preaching is not lifeless. It should be driven by God's presence and must lead others there. Nothing can ignite worship like Presence-Centered preaching—and nothing can defeat it more than humanistic oratory.

Be Listening

Every pastor knows the terror of Saturday night. That moment when it seems the heavens are brass and despite his best efforts, he has no clue what to say to the people the next morning. This is the agony of preaching. But the wise pastor has a prayer he prays early and often: "Lord, what do You want to say to Your People?"

That simple prayer, typed on a plain white strip of paper, has hung on my study wall over thirty years. To my absolute amazement, there has not been a time that I have cried out with that prayer in humble pleading that God has not graciously seemed to answer.

Is this because I'm really smart? Or homiletically gifted? Or a superb theologian? No. It's because God is more concerned about feeding His sheep than I am.

If you want to preach God's word, listen.

Be Prepared

The Bible is an amazing book. Everything we need for life and godliness is contained in its pages (2 Peter 1:2–4). It's the only book on earth that is literally alive (Hebrews 4:12). When opened, God speaks directly, authentically, and personally to us—if we will humbly listen.

So we must deal with the Scripture carefully. No casual, random approach to sermon preparation will do. Paul told Timothy he needed diligence to be "rightly dividing" the word of truth (2 Timothy 2:15 KJV). Paul, who doubled as a tentmaker, used a sewing term that means to "cut it straight."

"Don't deviate," Paul is saying to his young pastor-friend. "Stay right on the line with God's good pattern. It will turn out beautifully and everything will fit well!"

The wise pastor learns to study the text of his preaching fully and deeply. This is the spade work of preaching. Taking the tools, getting into the dirt, and discovering the gold. It's always there. Reading the text in multiple versions, recording observations, unpacking the words and their original meanings, discovering the full context of the passage and culture, and studying what great men have seen and recorded (commentaries), then pulling from your notes the central idea of the text: this is the weekly work of the faithful man of God.

When finished, you should know more about that passage than anyone in your congregation. But your work is not done.

The most joyous part of preaching involves prayerfully discovering what God wants the people to hear from the passage. You can't say everything you've learned. A local church gathering is not a seminary. Too much sideways information kills preaching. (Ask any church member who has thought, "What does that have to do with anything?")

"Lord, what do You want to say to Your people? And in what way do You want to say it?" This too is an art, learned through the years. How can we best explain this truth, illustrate this truth, and apply this truth to our hearers? How can they walk away having heard that single truth God is speaking to them in the power of His presence?

But the greatest goal in preaching is not merely discovering and delivering a teaching; it is encountering God Himself—and helping others also make that encounter.

Be Filled

As a college senior, I was afforded an amazing opportunity. A godly pastor I greatly respected was the president of our state denomination. As he was preparing the program for the annual denominational meeting, he took a massive risk and asked me to preach. It was the night they traditionally highlighted our Christian university.

I will never forget what Don Moore said with a serious smile and his finger pointed in my face. "Bill, I'm taking a great step of faith here. Don't you dare preach without being filled with the Holy Spirit!" Don knew his risk would be rewarded only if God showed up.

It's a tragedy for preaching to be boring. But it's even worse if the preacher is not filled with God. "Be filled with the Spirit," Paul exhorts, "speaking to one another . . ." (Ephesians 5:18–19). While the truth lies in the content of the message, the Spirit provides the fire.

It's easy for Christian leaders to slide into the tragic rut of "professional holiness." Like Samson, we know how to perform when the moment comes, but we play with sin throughout the week. Before our next responsibility, we quickly confess our sins, ask for God's help, and get up to deliver a message.

But we fail to understand that holiness has a cumulative nature. This doesn't mean we must be perfect; no one is. But intentional surrender throughout each day will yield increased understanding of God in the moments of delivery. God wants you to experience Him and the massaging of His message into your heart throughout the week. If you allow Him room, He will work the depth of the message into your soul in a way you can never achieve with a mere one-night preparation. A message prepared in a mind reaches a mind. But a message prepared in a life reaches a life.

And tragically, if "professional holiness" is your settled practice, you may one day have the experience of Samson.

"I will go out as at other times and shake myself free." But he did not know that the LORD had departed from him. (Judges 16:20).

Be Direct

God's Word is not given to entertain, but to transform. Not to inflate our minds, but to change our lives. So the good teacher of God's Word must ask his hearers probing questions: "What is God saying to you? And how will you respond?" He must not only display the menu, but also invite them to dine at the table. But first, these two questions must germinate in the heart of the preacher and find satisfactory answers. Then they will pierce with greater power into the hearts of the hearers, and they will cry out as they did with Peter's preaching, "What shall we do?" (Acts 2:37).

> *Charles Spurgeon was a third-generation preacher. It was said of his grandfather's preaching by a devout working-man, "He was always so experimental [experiential]. You felt as if he had been inside of a man."[5]*
>
> *For it is not mere words that nourish the soul, but God Himself, and unless and until the hearers find God in personal experience they are not the better for having heard the truth. The Bible is not an end in itself, but is meant to bring men to an intimate and satisfying knowledge of God, that they may enter into Him, that they may delight in His Presence, may taste and know the inner sweetness of the very God Himself in the core and center of their hearts.[6]*

Be Christ-Centered

What is the mystical difference in some preachers? Why do some shake you to your core, while others, at best, seem merely informative? Why do you leave some messages pleasantly educated—and others deeply moved?

Transforming preaching leads people to Christ and Christ alone. Study the text of Peter's messages. His one agenda was always to take his hearers through the foyer of God's conviction and grace into the presence of the living God. He knew that "There is salvation in no one else; for there is no other name under heaven that has been given among men by which we must be saved" (Acts 4:12).

> **Transforming preaching leads people to Christ and Christ alone.**

Paul determined to know nothing among men "except Jesus Christ, and Him crucified" (1 Corinthians 2:2). What did that really mean? If you had been under Paul's preaching, you would have left each encounter feeling you had been taken into the presence of the living God.
Our direction in each message must be, as Spurgeon said, to make a beeline to Christ. This doesn't mean a clumsily forced tagline on the end of the message, but a determination throughout to take people by the hand and help them encounter the One their soul longs for and desperately needs.

It's possible, as we plan our preaching, to become enamored with the message and not with Christ. We discover a good outline, a compelling illustration, and some clear transitions. It's fine to get wrapped up in the craft of exposition and delivery, but never to the exclusion of God's greatest agenda.

> I read Thy Word, O Lord, each passing day,
> and in the sacred page find glad employ.
> But this I pray:
> Save from the killing letter.
> Teach my heart, set free from human forms,
> the holy art of reading Thee in every line
> —in precept, prophecy, and sign—
> Till all my vision filled with Thee,
> Thy likeness shall reflect in me.
> Not knowledge, but Thyself my joy!
> For this I pray.[7]

We foster idolatry if people leave a sermon looking at us: our skill in handling the text, our wonderful oratory, our creative sermon design, our humorous anecdotes. We are commissioned to lead people to Christ! We should come down from every sermon, fall on our knees, and ask, "Did people encounter Christ? Were they introduced to Him? Did I deliberately and faithfully usher people to Him who alone can change their lives?" This should be our passion. It is what separates nice preaching from powerful preaching.

You are fearfully and wonderfully made, as God designed. I'm sure I'd be impressed to meet you. But lead your hearers to meet Jesus. They will never be the same.

LET THE BODY BREATH

Try this little experiment. Take a deep breath and hold it in . . . then never let it go. How's that work for you?

The church is Christ's body. As such, it needs to breathe. Both inhaling and exhaling are critical. Often our public gatherings are one dimensional. We sit and partake. We breathe in. But God's intent with His presence is not only for us to be filled, but also to overflow. Not only to take, but also to give.

Most leaders love to control a worship service. It's safe. All of us have experienced moments when someone went over the top in sharing a testimony or expressing their faith. But something is missing if we never let the body express itself in prayer, testimony, and response.

What would happen this Sunday morning if right after your message, you walked into the congregation with a microphone and asked, "What is God saying to you this morning?" You might be surprised what God was doing among His people—and the unique communications He was imparting to those He loves. If the rest of the body could hear that expression, more teaching, more application, and more worship might occur.

I'm not advocating this as a weekly exercise, but an illustration of how God might want to speak through other members of the body. Historically, the prayers and testimonies of God's people have invariably accompanied the greatest movements of revival. When people hear a pastor exhorting them, they expect such teaching. When a friend across the aisle gives a humble, broken testimony of what God is doing in their lives, suddenly every person realizes that God is real and available for them as well.

And prayer is breath: the breathing out of the soul to God. Many have been overwhelmed by the power of the Brooklyn Tabernacle in New York City, pastored by Jim Cymbala. Most intriguing are the Tuesday night prayer meetings, where thousands of people gather and cry out to God. The church is built on prayer. As Christian leaders have observed this church, many have tried to start a replica of their Tuesday night prayer meetings which thousands attend—with little success. Asked about this, Cymbala said, "I encourage pastors to start praying in their largest gathering of the week, which is usually their Sunday morning services. Preach a little less and open up the service to seasons of prayer and watch what God will do!"

Prayer should not be a perfunctory moment or a segue to the next song, but the constant inhaling and exhaling of the congregation in communion with God. As He directs, be sensitive in planning and even open up to the congregation for unhindered, shepherded seasons of testimoney and prayer.

HE'S WAITING

If Jesus were to hand-deliver a letter to your church, a fresh prescription for spiritual health, what would it say? We know, for He has given clear, representative letters to the seven churches of the Revelation.

At the close of His letter to the Laodicean church (who had drifted into soul-threatening pride and lukewarmness) Jesus ends with a gracious invitation.

> *Behold, I stand at the door and knock; if anyone hears My voice and opens the door, I will come in to him and will dine with him, and he with Me." (Revelation 3:20)*

He is waiting and knocking. Can you hear Him? Right outside the door of your church. Everything you need, He is and has. For everything flows from the presence of the Lord.

What will you do this week to open the door?

1. A.W. Tozer, The Pursuit of God, (Camp Hill, Penn.: Christian Publications, 1982), 108.

2. Merriam-Webster's Online Dictionary, 11th Edition, merrian-webster.com.

3. Tozer, The Pursuit of God, 26.

4. A.W. Tozer, The Pursuit of God, 9.

5. Charles Spurgeon, An Autobiography, (Harrington, Penn.: Delmarva Publications, 2013), location 936 in ebook (parenthesis added).

6. Tozer, "The Pursuit of God, 9.

7. J.C. Macauley, "Thyself."

7

EQUIP INTENTIONALLY

> *"Imagine yourself as a living house. God comes in to rebuild that house. At first, perhaps, you can understand what He is doing. He is getting the drains right and stopping the leaks in the roof and so on; you knew that those jobs needed doing and so you are not surprised. But presently He starts knocking the house about in a way that hurts abominably and does not seem to make any sense. What on earth is He up to? The explanation is that He is building quite a different house from the one you thought of—throwing out a new wing here, putting on an extra floor there, running up towers, making courtyards. You thought you were being made into a decent little cottage: but He is building a palace. He intends to come and live in it Himself."[1]*
>
> *C.S. Lewis*

Years ago, when the Soviet Union collapsed and opened their borders to outside missionaries, our church began to take teams of doctors into a city of over 300,000 people. Our doctors were eager to visit the hospitals and develop relationships that might open doors of ministry and witness in the medical community.

But what they discovered in one hospital astounded them. The beds had no sheets. There was no food. If you wanted bedding and food, you had to bring them yourself. A patient could literally starve to death. Worse, there was very little medicine. The doctors' prescription for almost any ailment was hydrotherapy: a few sessions in a whirlpool.

As our doctors toured the hospital alongside their foreign colleagues, they were impressed with the Russian doctors' passion, concern, and expertise. They were intelligent and gifted professionals. But they spoke frankly of their frustration with their inability to perform simple surgeries that could have been completed easily if they only had the right equipment. Whatever other Russian hospitals were like, this city was in dire medical need.

They lacked basic equipping, and people were dying needlessly. What could be worse?

TOOLS ARE IMPORTANT

Ask a carpenter, a teacher, a doctor, a housewife with a growing family, a computer technician. The lack of equipment can make someone's job difficult or impossible.

It's equally debilitating to have the right tools, but lack the know-how. Simple tasks that others accomplish easily become a struggle if you don't have the training.

When a person comes into a genuine relationship with Christ, they receive the raw empowering they need. Christ can do anything and He now lives in them. He is the essential equipment for living. But someone can go for years and fail to understand what it means to house the indwelling Christ and let Christ live through him.

A FRUSTRATING TESTIMONY WITH A HAPPY ENDING

I came to know Christ at age 7 and experienced a genuine conversion. I was overwhelmed with Christ in those early days. But like many, in my early teen years I was pulled by peer pressure into a lifestyle where Christ was not in control.

Along the way I came to the conclusion that the Christian life consisted of looking at what Jesus had done or might do, then trying to mimic Him. The only way this seemed feasible was to try to live in my own strength. As beloved as the classic book (In His Steps) was to many, it seemed to confirm my beliefs. Look at Him and do what He's doing . . . the best you can.

So I tried . . . and tried . . . and tried . . . and tried. I would make vows that were quickly broken. Habitual sins flooded into my life during my early teen years (with my full cooperation) and I found I was powerless to overcome them. Every day I went further into a spiritual deficit.

At age 12 I had received a strong call from the Lord to preach. (God had to get my attention early!) This call never wavered in my young teenage heart. But how could I possibly preach with such defeat? Who would want what I had?

In retrospect, I believe the Lord let me struggle in this Bill-Elliff-Self-Help program to engrain forever in me something I might have learned no other way: I was bankrupt. Helpless. Unable to live the Christian life on my own. My best effort was useless. He was teaching me the full force of Jesus' statement in John 15:5: "Apart from Me you can do nothing."

On April 4, 1969, I came to the end of myself. In a church service where God was present, I gave up. "Lord," I cried in prayer, "If you want to do anything with my life, You're going to have to do it. I can't. I fully surrender my life to You."

That was just what God was waiting for: the recognition of my total spiritual poverty, combined with glad surrender. In the following days, the heavens seem to open. I had not known such joy and freedom since the first days of my salvation.

Quickly, under the instruction of my pastor-father, I spent time confessing my sin and clearing my conscience with the many I'd sinned against. At the exact same time, I was exposed to some teaching that helped me understand that at the moment of my conversion, the Spirit of God had literally come to indwell me! This was an absolutely new thought—the most liberating news.

My brother, Jim, had come to this understanding a few months before. Together we began to study the Scripture, read helpful literature, and listen to great men of God on cassette recordings. I remember often driving across the state to hear men preach on these themes.

Three months later, a powerful missionary came home to furlough at our church. Bud Fray had been used all across Rhodesia (now

Zimbabwe). Bud had felt called to ministry under my father's pastorate in a small, South Arkansas town and had a great passion for discipling young believers.

He had one request for the summer of his furlough: He wanted to take any high school students who were interested and teach them every week about the Spirit-filled life. For three months, about a dozen of us sat at his feet. I don't know about the others, but the equipping I received from Bud Fray transformed me.

The equipping I gained that year from my brothers, my dad, and multiple teachers (both live and by recording), changed the trajectory of my life. One of the most powerful things was learning how to read the Word daily, record what God was saying, then aggressively cooperate with God by following the promptings of His Spirit and the illumination of His Word. This set me on a path of personal equipping that would feed me for the rest of my life. Those days of discipling gave me the tools and the know-how for spiritual living.

THE GLORIOUS GOAL
Draw a mental line across the room you're sitting in. At one end place an unbelieving seeker of Christ. At the other, position that same person and envision them as a fully devoted, fully equipped follower of Jesus. Then see if you can answer two critical questions:

- What does a fully devoted follower of Jesus look like?
- How do they get there?

If you don't know the answers, you may not only fail to never grow to spiritual maturity and usefulness yourself, but also never take anyone else with you. This would be, in my opinion, the tragic description of a wasted life.

The apostle Paul knew the answers and he made them the topic of most of his letters to the churches. Look at two of his greatest statements, penned under the inspiration of the Spirit of God.

> *And He gave some as apostles, and some as prophets, and some as evangelists, and some as pastors and teachers, for the equipping of the saints for the work of service, to the*

building up of the body of Christ; until we all attain to
the unity of the faith, and of the knowledge of the Son of
God, to a mature man, to the measure of the stature which
belongs to the fullness of Christ. (Ephesians 4:11-13)

Of this church I was made a minister according to the
stewardship from God bestowed on me for your benefit, so
that I might fully carry out the preaching of the word of
God, that is, the mystery which has been hidden from the
past ages and generations, but has now been manifested
to His saints, to whom God willed to make known what is
the riches of the glory of this mystery among the Gentiles,
which is Christ in you, the hope of glory. We proclaim Him,
admonishing every man and teaching every man with all
wisdom, so that we may present every man complete in
Christ. For this purpose also I labor, striving according to
His power, which mightily works within me.
(Colossians 1:25–29)

Remember those years when your mom backed you up to the
doorframe to place a small mark and record your height? You stood as
tall as you could, and you were thrilled the next year when the mark
was two inches higher!

Now, place Christ against the doorframe. Look for a moment at the
"measure of the stature" of Christ in all His fullness. What do you see?
Some amazing attributes: Full love, joy, peace, and patience. Wisdom
and knowledge. Passion. You also see some stunning activity: worship,
growth, ministry, mission, giving. In short, you see a complete man. A
man as man was intended: full of the glory of God!

That's the goal for you and for every person God brings across your
path. Paul understood this, which is why he labored according to
God's power working through him to help every man grow up to
completeness in Christ.

Paul knew that potential lay in every true believer because of "Christ
in [them], the hope of glory!" Paul's main agenda was to help believers
experience and depend upon the Christ who now lived within them.

All we need is in us because Christ is in us and He wants to be released through our mortal bodies. He has planned for us, in a way unlike anything else in creation, to display the glory of God.

THE PROBLEM

So why the disconnect? Why, after our salvation, aren't we instantly like Jesus? As one man said, it's our "earth-suit." We are limited by our body (with all its weaknesses) and our soul (which through the years we have overly relied on and wrongly trained). Our soul encompasses our mind, with which we think; our emotions, with which we feel; and our wills, with which we decide. Before the Spirit comes to dwell within, our body and soul are our only resource for living. They're all we've got.

When we become followers of Christ, our soul is not immediately changed. The Word instructs us that over time our mind must be renewed, our emotions tamed, and our will increasingly broken and surrendered to Him. "Not my will, but Thine be done" needs to become our constant prayer.

When we receive Christ, His Spirit comes to live in us. This gives us a new internal power. Suddenly we have the engine that's been missing from our car.

We must learn to move from operating on the soulish, carnal level to the Spirit level. Christ lives in us, but we must learn to live from the inside out, letting His Spirit fill us and flow through us like "rivers of living water" (John 7:37–39). It takes time to learn how to live consistently in dependence on this new operating system.

Ron Dunn, a wonderful pastor and Bible teacher who is now in heaven, was once trying to drive in Scotland with his wife. The Scottish drive on the opposite side of the road than Americans. Ron said he was doing fine until he stopped at a traffic light waiting to turn while he and his wife were talking. When he turned the corner, he automatically moved to the right-hand side of the road.

He looked up and saw a car barreling toward him. He said to Kay, "Look at that idiot in my lane."

"Wrong idiot," she said. "Move over!"

Ron hadn't intended to drive in the wrong lane, but he had driven on the right-hand side so long, he automatically moved in that direction.

If we have lived in dependence on ourselves, it takes time and training to learn how to rely—every moment of every day—on the Spirit and let Him lead.

THE CONTENT OF DISCIPLESHIP

We don't have to look far for Christ's exhortation to help people live in this new way. Jesus gave us a mission that is so clear anyone can understand it, yet so profound it will take us a lifetime to complete our part. He simply said, "Make disciples, baptize them, and train them."

> Our greatest goal in discipling believers is to help them live in Christ—and equip them to do the same with others.

We call Matthew 28:18–20 the Great Co-Mission because it's Christ and us together. We are called to lead people to a saving relationship with Christ, then help them experience and enjoy Christ, who now lives within. Our greatest goal in discipling believers is to help them live in Christ—and equip them to do the same with others.

Right after Christ gave this all-encompassing commission and before His ascension to heaven, the disciples were told to wait in Jerusalem for the promised Holy Spirit. On the day of Pentecost, He came to indwell each of their lives, giving them the needed power to do their assignment. We find in Acts 2 that as they began to walk in the fullness of the Spirit, the world could easily see their Christ-filled lifestyles: what a fully devoted follower looked and acted like. Perhaps the most succinct and beautiful snapshot of the church comes at the close of Acts 2.

> *They were continually devoting themselves to the apostles'*
> *teaching and to fellowship, to the breaking of bread and*
> *to prayer. Everyone kept feeling a sense of awe; and many*
> *wonders and signs were taking place through the apostles.*
> *And all those who had believed were together and had all*
> *things in common; and they began selling their property*
> *and possessions and were sharing them with all, as anyone*

> might have need. Day by day continuing with one mind
> in the temple, and breaking bread from house to house,
> they were taking their meals together with gladness and
> sincerity of heart, praising God and having favor with all
> the people. And the Lord was adding to their number day
> by day those who were being saved. (Acts 2:42–47)

As they walked in the fullness of His Spirit, we see the spiritual **attributes** that would later be identified by Paul in Galatians 5:22–23 as the "fruit" that the Spirit produces when He is in control: *love, joy, peace, patience, kindness, goodness, faithfulness, gentleness, and self-control.*

Almost effortlessly, as they followed the Spirit, they fell into a lifestyle of at least six daily **activities**: *worship, community, growth, ministry, missions, and giving.*

When people walk in the power of the Spirit, they look like Christ because Christ is pouring through their lives. The fruit of the Spirit is evident. When Christ is in control, they are led to **worship** God, engage in loving **community, grow** spiritually, **minister** in the realm of their unique gifts, give their lives to the compelling **mission** of reaching and training others (at home and around the world), and **give** with hilarious generosity. This is what a fully devoted Christ-follower looks like.

If you long to develop a Presence-Centered church, help people see this glorious picture of their destiny. But consistently remind them that this is possible only as they live on the Spirit-led level. This all springs from the presence of Christ within them.

THE CULTURE OF DISCIPLESHIP

So how can we help people experience Christ in these ways? Become Acts 2 Christians, living in Acts 2 community?

> Discipleship must become the accepted culture, not an anomaly.

Healthy churches develop a discipling culture like that seen in the early church. We need concentric circles of environments (as we talked about in Chapter 5) where Christ is experienced and the processes to Spirit-controlled living are explained. But most of all we need every maturing believer, beginning with the leaders, to embrace their lifelong task of personally training others. We need people like Bud Fray all over the church who love others and will pour into them. Discipleship must become the accepted culture, not an anomaly.

We must help people see that no believer is exempt from discipling, and no believer is unable to disciple others, because Christ is in them. Every believer must be growing up to the understanding that it's their job to help those around them learn to walk in Christ. This is why they live—and it can become their greatest joy! Every true believer wants a ministry, and whatever else they're doing, this is every believer's ministry.

Can I load you up with a long sentence to help us see what equipping is all about?

> *We must help people experience Jesus by giving them the pattern of sound words in both basic and advanced on-the-job training, with usable tools, in concentric relational environments, all the time, with multiplication in mind!*

Let's break that down:

• *We must help people experience Jesus . . .*

The goal of all equipping is not to give people a system or a new religious paradigm to follow. It's to help them encounter Christ. All our discipling must be aimed at bringing people into increasing intimacy with Him, because everything flows from the presence of the Lord!

Our constant question to those we train should be: "Are you experiencing Christ today? Was He noticeably present today in your life at work, at home, at play? If not, what was hindering the flow of Christ through your life?"

We must help them see that every problem is an opportunity to encounter Christ. And every solution is ultimately found in Christ's presence. Our discipling of others must be an unceasing attempt to lead them back to Christ.

• We must help people experience Jesus **by giving them the pattern of sound words . . .**

You can imagine that as Paul trained men, he got better and better at the process. Over the years he learned what men needed and began to develop his own way to teach men how to walk by the Spirit. As you study his letters to the churches, you notice some patterns of how he communicated these truths.

This is why he told one of his disciples, young Timothy, to "retain the standard [the pattern] of sound words which you have heard from me, in the faith and love which are in Christ Jesus" (2 Timothy 1:13). This is important for each believer and each church. There are multiple ways to communicate the primary truths of the gospel and the basics of Christian living. The truths themselves are unchangeable, but the ways of expressing them can be uniquely tailored through the grid of each believer's personality and communication style.

Church leaders must never assume their people know how to disciple others. Every church will help its people if they began to formulate a primary means of communicating the gospel and the basics of how to walk by the Spirit. This becomes the common, transferable language that gives easy "on ramps" in discipling others.

> Church leaders must never assume their people know how to disciple others.

Over the years, people will come to understand a lifestyle of worship, community, growth, missions, ministry, and giving—then speak of it in similar terms. They not only know what it is, but they also know how to explain it to those they're discipling. Then their disciples can transfer it to their own disciples.

Not long ago, our staff spent a semester reading multiple times through all of Paul's letters to discover the "pattern of sound words" he taught his disciples. We wanted to discover the content that Paul was pouring into his disciples.

We identified at least nine key truths for Christian living and behavior that we began to teach our people. It has become a helpful discipling tool.

THE PATTERN

- *The glory of God is our motivation.*
- *Christ is our message.*
- *Discipling all people is our mission.*
- *The surrendered life is our manner.*
- *The Spirit of God is our might.*
- *The Word of God and prayer are our means.*
- *Using our gifts in love is our ministry.*
- *The church is our method.*
- *Eternity is our mindset!*

Regardless how it is worded or developed, you must understand the basics of Christian living and equip people with these truths. You must give them the pattern of sound words as they are given to us in Scripture.

*We must help people experience Jesus by giving them the pattern of sound words **in basic** . . .*

To aid this understanding, every church would be well served by some intentional, basic training. Don't leave new converts or new attenders in the dark about the glorious life to which Christ has called them and how it can be experienced.

Teach such areas as how to be released from the baggage of our past, how to be filled with the Holy Spirit, how to grow spiritually through the Word and prayer, and how to begin to lead others to Christ and help them grow. Explain the Spirit-led *attributes* of a fully devoted follower and their *lifestyle habits.* This happens most effectively through one-on-one and group contexts.

*We must help people experience Jesus by giving them the pattern of sound words in basic **and advanced** . . .*

Wise leaders will develop continual training as needed in many areas. Learning how to walk with Christ is a lifelong process. There is a reason the Bible contains sixty-six books of example and instruction. We need every page!

Paul told his disciples that "All Scripture is inspired by God and profitable for teaching, for reproof, for correction, for training in righteousness; so that the man of God may be adequate, equipped for every good work" (2 Timothy 3:16–17). Rick Warren says the Word is good for teaching (shows us the path), reproof (shows us when we get off the path), correction (shows us how to get back on the path), and training (shows us how to stay on the path). We can never get enough of God's Word. It is the foundation for all training.

One of our greatest steps of equipping will be to show disciples how to study the Bible. We once did a survey with twenty godly men in our church. We listed the multiple ways we can be equipped, then had them rank what had been most significant in their growth. Each said their primary means of growth was their daily, personal study of God's Word.

Great disciplers know their first task is to teach others how to read, study, and apply the Word. It's the old adage of giving a man a fish versus teaching him how to fish. One gets fed for a day; the other can feed himself for a lifetime. The rest of their lives will be spent learning more and more of Christ through His Word and helping others do the same!

> Great disciplers know their first task is to teach others how to read, study, and apply the Word.

We must help people experience Jesus by giving them the pattern of sound words in basic and advanced **on-the-job training . . .**

Any employer will tell you the most valuable development comes in on-the-job training with a gifted trainer. Great disciplers look for ministry and service opportunities to bring their disciples along. They push their disciples to lead others to Christ. They challenge them into positions where they must have the Spirit's empowering. They encourage them to take steps of faith, to engage in ministry, to serve others.

This is why a ministry opportunity or mission trip can give spiritual growth such a great jump-start. It's a time of concentrated ministry with gifted disciplers in an environment that demands faith.

If you are genuinely intent on making disciples, never do anything without a disciple by your side! Make a habit to take others along—and don't assume they understand all they need to know about life or ministry. They are with you both to serve and to learn, so seize the opportunity.

*We must help people experience Jesus by giving them the pattern of sound words in basic and advanced on-the-job training, **with usable tools . . .***

People need practical handles. If our primary task is to make disciples, do you know how to do that—and how to teach others to do the same? What tools will you use that are reproducable and transferable?

As you study how Jesus and Paul discipled people, you notice not only a pattern in the *content* of their discipling, but also their *method.*

In our church, we have identified this as the Big 5 of Paul's discipling. These were methods he used over and over with those he trained. We developed a simple model and questions people could use as they met weekly with people they were developing. We trained our people how to use this simple method, which gives them a framework for discipling conversations and engagement.

THE BIG 5

> **Care:** "How's your heart?"
> **Accountability:** "How's your progress?"
> **Vision-Casting:** "What's your next step?"
> **Truth:** "What is God teaching you from His Word?"
> **Prayer:** "What can we pray for right now?"

You may create another method for training others in how to disciple. There are many possible tools. The point is this: *People need practical tools to learn what to do and how to live!* If we are going to equip them, we must give them good tools to use.

*We must help people experience Jesus by giving them the pattern of sound words in basic and advanced on-the-job training, with usable tools, **in concentric relational environments . . .***

As we saw in Chapter 5, Jesus' discipling was never done in just one environment with just one approach. Discipleship happens with many people in many environments. The secret to most great disciplers is that they are *looking for every opportunity* to pour into the lives of those God brings across their paths.

Sometimes they will meet daily with those they're discipling. Sometimes it's a single conversation in a week. Sometimes it's helping them get under public teaching or into a small group. Sometimes it's private study. Sometimes it's encouraging them to read a great book or listen to a certain podcast. Always it's seizing the teachable moment. The goal is to use every means possible to help people experience the presence of Christ and learn from Him.

Our investment in a person may be a single encounter, or it may stretch over years. But our goal should be to lead everyone to experience the presence of Christ. We are to "proclaim Him, admonishing every man and teaching every man with all wisdom, so that we may present every man complete in Christ" (Colossians 1:28).

Years ago when I traveled with Life Action Ministries, we were in services almost every night. Often, when I would sense that God was wanting to manifest Himself during a service, I would bring one or more of my children in from their children's clubs so they could experience those moments.

One particular night, I was impressed to bring my 8-year-old son into the service. God showed up in power and I could almost feel God speaking to my son. Soon I heard him sniffling and he tugged on my shirt asking me if I'd go with him to the prayer room where he burst into tears.

"Dad, God is calling me to preach," he said. He knew and I knew. Did Dad call him to preach? Heaven forbid! My goal was just to get him into the environment of God's presence so he could be discipled more deeply. God is fully capable of speaking to an 8-year-old. Today as I write these words, my son is preaching and planting a new church.

Our goal should be to expose our disciples to as many relational environments and ministry opportunities as possible so they can encounter Jesus in multiple ways!

*We must help people experience Jesus by giving them the pattern of sound words in basic and advanced on-the-job training, with usable tools, in concentric relational environments, **all the time** . . .*

A discipling culture is filled with people who never miss a moment to invest in others. They know how to seize discipleship along the way. Discipling is not about a thirteen-week study. That may be a component of equipping. But discipling is something done all the time.

A great way to see this is to look inside our own home.

Our first disciples are in our family. This is God's training ground, not only for young disciples, but also for moms and dads as disciplers. It makes sense that discipling others should be modeled after the process God gives us to disciple our children. Any good parent knows that training must be done *every day along the way.*

> *These words, which I am commanding you today, shall be on your heart. You shall teach them diligently to your sons and shall talk of them when you sit in your house and when you walk by the way and when you lie down and when you rise up. You shall bind them as a sign on your hand and they shall be as frontals on your forehead. You shall write them on the doorposts of your house and on your gates. (Deuteronomy 6:6–9)*

I have often said that if I find a godly mom or dad who has learned how to effectively (not perfectly) disciple their children, they can easily disciple others.

Don't view the equipping of others as a mere Bible study, but as an ongoing, frequent investment of your life in theirs. My granddad often said, "You ain't taught until they've learned!" We must keep at it to help those we love become fully devoted followers of Jesus!

*We must help people experience Jesus by giving them the pattern of sound words in basic and advanced on-the-job training, with usable tools, in concentric relational environments, all the time, **with multiplication in mind!***

Every church leader must be a disciple and must see their lifelong goal to equip others, who will equip others. The endgame of discipleship is not just to help a single man or woman. It is to help others, who will help others, who will help others, who will help others. Notice the four generations of disciples I've marked in Paul's admonition to young Timothy:

> The things which **you** [Timothy] have heard from **me** [Paul] in the presence of many witnesses, entrust these to faithful **men** [Timothy's disciples] who will be able to teach **others** also [Timothy's disciples' disciples!] (2 Timothy 2:2)

The power of multiplication is astounding. Do the math on what happens when you disciple someone who will then disciple someone else. The first year you disciple one person and the following year you both disciple one person . . . and you continue this cycle. In twenty years, you would disciple more than 1 million people! The results are exponential.

This is God's plan and always has been. How could Christ entrust the growth of the church to a ragtag band of 120 people on a hillside and expect to change the world? Two things made this possible: the power of the Holy Spirit and the principle of spiritual multiplication.

It worked! As we are discipling someone, we must always keep multiplication in mind and cast to them the vision of being a lifelong discipler of disciple-makers!

I love that Christ did not give us a one-size-fits-all regimen for equipping others. He gave us an unmistakable calling and a book that's alive and powerful and filled with truth to discover and share. He showed us models all around us through human history who have humbly and faithfully invested in others.

Most of all, He came to live in us, making it possible for us to "know Him and the power of His resurrection" (Philippians 3:10). He gave us all the power we need to live and help others live! And He gave us a multiplying plan that ensures we can have a legacy that affects generations. We get to be a part of the ongoing movement to redeem the world! But we must engage in discipling others. If we will, the rewards are beyond imagination.

A STUNNING STORY

Picture the scene. Earth as we know it has ended. Everything has been accomplished, just as God has planned. It is time for the handing out of rewards to God's children. All of God's heavenly order has assembled. The stands are filled with myriads of angels in brilliant array. The floor of the massive hall contains every believer from every age stretching as far as the eye can see.

At the end of the hall is the Great White Throne with One seated on it and the Son of God seated at His right hand.

The hall cannot keep silent. One being after another break out in glorious praise as they gaze upon the throne. Sounds from this arena have never been heard on earth: choruses of thunderous praise and quiet moments that steal each one's breath.

After a long season of worship (for we have all of eternity) the Father lifts His hand and declares the moment has come to begin the rewards. A hush falls on the crowd, but a slow murmur of questions runs through the great hall. "Who will the Great One call first? What will they receive?"

Then the Lord of Glory calls His beloved servant, Paul. "Paul, come forward."

The faithful missionary humbly approaches the throne. A ripple of excitement stirs through the crowd.

The Lord places His omnipotent hand upon his servant and turns him to face the crowd.

"Let us begin," He says.

On perfect cue, a young man stands among the billions, miraculously able to be heard by everyone.

"Paul," he says, "Do you remember me? I'm Timothy, your young son in the faith. Remember the time you talked to me late in the night as

I turned my heart to Christ? The long hours we walked together? The days we poured over the Scripture and you taught me of the indwelling Christ? How you taught me as a young man to overcome my fears?

"Remember, Paul, how we served together and experienced the Lord's presence invading our meetings, changing lives over and over again? You taught me almost everything I know.

"I am here, Paul, by God's grace, through your discipling life. And here are others—those I led to Christ and those they led to Christ." A ripple swells into a mighty wave across the arena as tens, then thousands, then millions slowly stand.

"I just want to say, 'Thank you, my dear father in the faith!'"

The stadium erupts with hallelujahs and singing. It continues for what seems hours as each believer remembers the blessed experiences of their salvation and is awed once again by the amazing ways God came to them through humble friends. They cannot wait to tell their stories.

Then the Lord silences them.

A woman stands.

"Paul, do you remember me? I am Lydia. While others passed us by, you looked for someone you felt might be seeking God down by the water. You explained to us Christ's death and resurrection. You gave us the glorious news of life in Him. It was just a single encounter, but I am here, in great measure, Paul, because of you! And here (others begin to stand) are my children and children's children and their children—entire generations—who are here because of God's grace as it came through you. Thank you, Paul!"

> Who knows what floods through generations from one discipling life?

This goes on for hours. Days. Who knows what floods through generations from one discipling life?

And at the perfect moment, the humbled, radiant servant feels God's hand upon his shoulder, turning him to face the Great Throne, and he hears these words:

"Well done! You are my good and faithful servant! You fought the good fight and finished the course and now, enter into the joy I have prepared for you!"

And Paul remembers what he himself had written under the Spirit's guiding hand to those he had discipled in Thessalonica.

> *For who is our hope or joy or crown of exultation?*
> *Is it not even you, in the presence of our Lord Jesus at His*
> *coming? For you are our glory and joy!*
> *(1 Thessalonians 2:19–20)*

And it will be . . . *enough!*

---

1. C.S. Lewis, The Weight of Glory, (New York: The MacMillan Co., 1949), 14–15.

8

ENGAGE PASSIONATELY

> *"Lo, I am with you always, even to the end of the age.'*
> *There is a realization of Christ's Presence which can be*
> *enjoyed only by those who personally or corporately fulfill*
> *this evangelistic commission."* [1]
>
> *Stephen Olford*

I love Christmas. Almost everything about it (except the shopping) pleases me. The music, the decorations, the smells, the extra attention we give each other, the joy of children and grandchildren, the special services that highlight the birth of Christ. It's a sweet and precious time.

But several years ago, while preparing a series of messages for the Christmas season from Isaiah 9, I came to see Christmas very differently. Christmas is not about warm, fuzzy sentimentalism. It was a military invasion. The greatest in all history.

> *The people who walk in darkness will see a great light;*
> *Those who live in a dark land, the light will shine on them.*
>
> *You shall multiply the nation, You shall increase their*
> *gladness; They will be glad in Your presence as with the*
> *gladness of harvest, As men rejoice when they divide the*
> *spoil.*
>
> *For You shall break the yoke of their burden and the staff on*
> *their shoulders, The rod of their oppressor, as at the battle*
> *of Midian.*

> *For every boot of the booted warrior in the battle tumult,*
> *And cloak rolled in blood, will be for burning, fuel for*
> *the fire.*
>
> *For a child will be born to us, a son will be given to us;*
> *And the government will rest on His shoulders; And His*
> *name will be called Wonderful Counselor, Mighty God,*
> *Eternal Father, Prince of Peace.*
>
> *There will be no end to the increase of His government or*
> *of peace, on the throne of David and over his kingdom, To*
> *establish it and to uphold it with justice and righteousness*
> *from then on and forevermore. The zeal of the LORD of*
> *hosts will accomplish this. (Isaiah 9: 2–7)*

Two thousand years ago, a Warrior-King who was both fully God and fully man broke into human history with a single agenda and He would not be denied. He came into the darkness and bondage of this world to deliver people—to set them free and establish a new government that would never end. A kingdom where He alone would reign as Sovereign, forever and ever. All who would believe and follow could be included.

At the beginning of His ministry, His archenemy met Him in the wilderness—twisting, turning, and deceiving—to divert the Warrior from His mission. But Christ was too wise. He knew His battle and His weapons. He took the sword of the Spirit, which is the Word of God, and dispatched His Enemy. The wretched cur retreated until a more opportune time.

Jesus began to announce what the new government would be like and how people could enter. It was paradise regained, and the entrance was open to every man or woman, boy or girl who would recognize their spiritual poverty and bow with glad surrender before this gracious Sovereign.

Every battle plan was in place to accomplish the deliverance. The final blow against the Enemy came unsuspected through the sacrificial death of the Warrior-King to pay for the sins of the people before a holy God. Satan laughed for three days . . . until Christ burst forth from the grave. Death was no match for the Master.

All along the way, Jesus had reminded his growing band of followers why He came. He was laser-focused on His military mission:

> For the Son of Man has come to seek and to save that
> which was lost." (Luke 19:10)

Like any good commander, the Father had given one direct, unmistakable call to His Warrior-Son: "Go get our family!" Simple as that. And the Son of God was not about to disappoint His Father.

ENLISTED AND ENGAGED

All of us who have been bought with the price of Christ's blood are now in this army. Until the final engagement is complete, we are also under clear marching orders. Impelled by our Warrior-King's calling and empowered by His Spirit, we are to seek and save the lost. Everybody, everywhere, all the time.

Over the course of five decades, I have observed many churches. I've seen vibrant churches and dead churches. Intentional churches and clueless churches. But one thing remains abundantly clear: Christ is uniquely present in places where His people are engaged in His mission! He knows He is needed there—and that His comrades-in-arms cannot fulfill their job without His presence. "Lo, I am with you always, even to the end of the age" was not a sentimental tagline to Matthew 28:20, but a General's promise given at His troops' commissioning.

> Christ is uniquely present in places where His people are engaged in His mission!

If you want to be a church alive with the presence of God, go where He's going: in your neighborhood and around the world. Jesus is there when His church enters the battle for the lives He loves. But if you're not interested in what interests Jesus, don't expect His presence to be powerfully manifested.

So what will help us engage in the mission? What will invite His presence?

Constant Reminding

It's incredibly easy to forget our mission or grow weary in the battle. So leaders who long for a church of God's presence stir up their people by example and exhortation. Keep evangelism and missions in the forefront. Use every opportunity in teaching to remind people of the mission.

Never portray evangelistic engagement as drudgery or duty. Those who engage wholeheartedly discover that joining with the Spirit in leading people to Christ is their deepest joy and privilege. What could be greater than being Christ's feet to run to those in slavery, Christ's arms to lift people from their bondage, and Christ's mouth to proclaim good news and introduce others to the Captain of our salvation?

Regular preaching and teaching, weekly illustrations and testimonies, and commissionings as you send people out on mission trips and reports from the mission field or church-planting leaders: use any way that God initiates to keep the mission before the army.

We must help believers, as they walk in the Spirit, to see people as Jesus sees them. People apart from God (even the most sinful) are not objects of evangelism, but fearfully and wonderfully made beings who could one day rule and reign with Christ.

C.S. Lewis reminds us how we should see and deal with everyone around us:

> It is a serious thing to live in a society of gods and goddesses, to remember that the dullest and most uninteresting person you talk to may one day be a creature which, if you saw it now, you would be strongly tempted to worship, or else a horror and a corruption such as you now meet, if at all, only in a nightmare. All day long we are, in some degree, helping each other to one or other of these destinations.
>
> It is in the light of these overwhelming possibilities, it is with the awe and the circumspection proper to them, that we should conduct all our dealings with one another, all friendships, all loves, all play, all politics. There are no ordinary people. You have never talked to a mere mortal.[2]

Constant Equipping

Peter was the apostle who found himself unprepared for his greatest window for witness. It happened the night of Christ's trial. Fueled by fear and the chaos of the moment, he fumbled the chance to boldly proclaim Christ.

This wise leader would never again let this happen. We see him several weeks later ready to speak, and 3,000 people were saved. His letter to others who were facing persecution reminds them of the need for good preparation:

> But even if you should suffer for the sake of righteousness, you are blessed. And do not fear their intimidation, and do not be troubled, but sanctify Christ as Lord in your hearts, always being ready to make a defense to everyone who asks you to give an account for the hope that is in you, yet with gentleness and reverence; and keep a good conscience so that in the thing in which you are slandered, those who revile your good behavior in Christ will be put to shame. (1 Peter 3:14–16)

"Let Christ fill your heart," Peter says, "and be always ready to tell people about Jesus." Always ready.

Alongside our exhortations to evangelism and missions, we should give continual training. Anything and everything, in every environment possible, to "equip the saints to do the work" of leading others to Christ. No child of God from your church should be able to say in eternity, "Lord, I just didn't know it was my mission and I never had an opportunity to learn how to seek and to save the lost."

Are you prepared? If someone asked you, right now, about the hope that is within you, could you share the gospel and lead that person to Him? There are hundreds of tools available. But you must make the effort to learn and use them. A soldier headed to the battlefield knows his life and the lives of those around him may depend on his readiness. He prepares. He works in anticipation of the battle so that when it comes, his responses are second nature.

Christ is ever-present to the believer who wants to share Him with others. He even says He will supply the words needed and certainly the power. But we most often use what we know. If you are a Christian leader, train your people in the gospel. You are a soldier of Christ! So give yourself aggressively to the training.

Constant Dependence

The great pastor Stephen Olford says, "There was a time in my life when the thought of talking with people, publicly or privately paralyzed me with fear."[3] He then recounts what led to the discovery of what he calls the secret of soul-winning:

> *God sovereignly stepped in. He had permitted me to struggle on long enough to convince me that I could no nothing about it. I was shy. I was bound; and I was defeated. In a word, I was a failure.*
>
> *Divinely ordered circumstances were used to bring me out of the bondage of soul-winning in the flesh, into the blessing of soul-winning in the Spirit . . . I began to see— slowly but clearly—that soul-winning is God's work. From the start to the finish He must plan and carry it through.*
>
> *My business is to be in line with the will of God. Winning men and women to the Lord Jesus Christ is not a matter of trial and error, but of being led by the Spirit . . . The Lord Jesus is the only successful soul-winner, and it is only when He is in complete control of my life that I can hope to share in the fruits of His labor."[4]*

Most believers know they should be involved in evangelism. Often we have made feeble, unsuccessful attempts. We must understand that true evangelism occurs as we trust the Spirit within us to lead, empower, and do His work—through us—to bring people to Himself. Then we leave the results to Him and give Him the glory when lives are changed. It is the Spirit's job (not ours) to convince the lost of their sin, Christ's righteousness, and the coming judgment and to draw men to Christ (John 16:8).

Constant Spirituality

Those who long to be engaged in God's mission must walk daily with Christ in the power of the Holy Spirit. Although no one does this perfectly, we must be vigilant, refusing anything that would quench or grieve His Spirit. We must realize the direct correlation between maturing holiness and mission effectiveness.

Since only Christ can save the unbelieving and we do not know when or where that will occur, we must let Him control our lives at all times, leading us and releasing through us the sweet fragrance of His presence.

> *There is a certain . . . impressiveness of character which attaches to a profound spirituality, and which is commandingly present in those who walk in the fellowship of the Holy Ghost. I know not how to define it. It is a certain convincing aroma, self-witnessing, like the perfume of a flower.*
>
> *It is independent of mental equipment . . . It works without the aid of speech because it is the effluence of a silent and secret communion. It begins to minister before you preach; it continues its ministry when the sermon is ended. It is endowed with marvelous powers of compulsion, and it sways the lives of others when mere words would miserably fail.*[5]

Constant Intercession

We'll discover much more about this in the next chapter, but remember that Jesus faced His greatest opposition from the Enemy when He was seeking and saving the lost. Jesus was in constant communion with the Father. He would get up "in the early morning, while it was still dark" to pray and sometimes spend whole nights in prayer (Mark 1:35). Why? As a man, He needed the presence, wisdom, and empowering of His Father for the great task. And He knew that prayer brings God into the equation.

The only One who can save people is God. We can (and must) cooperate with Him, but in the end it is His presence and power that saves them. How could we possibly expect to be successful without crying out to the only Savior for His intervention in the lives of those He loves?

One of the most bone-chilling passages in the Bible is Paul's battlefield description of the enemies we face:

> For our struggle is not against flesh and blood, but against
> the rulers, against the powers, against the world forces of
> this darkness, against the spiritual forces of wickedness in
> the heavenly places. (Ephesians 6:12)

Read that again slowly. If you can read that without some fear creeping up your spine, you are bolder than I am! You have two choices. You can be naïve about this and pay the price and make little progress in the gospel. Our you can realize this is written to warn us and drive us to prayer. We have an Enemy. He has a mission, and it diametrically opposes ours. In fact, his mission is to abort ours: to stop the advance of the Kingdom of God.

At one time, we had a highly decorated Green Beret in our church. He was a Viet Nam veteran. He told me that before every mission, his unit would go into a lockdown for a week. One of their main tasks was to study the enemy so they would know more about him than he knew about himself. They wanted to remove any element of surprise regarding the enemy's behavior.

Our Commander wants us to know our enemy and use the means necessary for his defeat. The beautiful thing about Paul's exhortation in Ephesians 6 is that it's surrounded by reminders that we can overcome our Enemy. It is a battle, but it's winnable. We can "be strong" against the Enemy in the "strength of [God's] might" (Ephesians 6:10). We have the provision of the whole armor of God. But everything builds in this passage to the final admonition. Paul's greatest tool in this battle is prayer:

> With **all** prayer and petition pray at **all** times in the Spirit,
> and with this in view, be on the alert with **all** perseverance
> and petition for **all** the saints, and pray on my behalf, that
> utterance may be given to me in the opening of my mouth,
> to make known with boldness the mystery of the gospel, for
> which I am an ambassador in chains; that in proclaiming
> it I may speak boldly, as I ought to speak.
> (Ephesians 6:18–20 *emphasis added*)

Notice the four "alls" in those verses. Mark this in your boot camp training manual and underline it: *This mission will not go well without prayer!* If you try to do this on your own, you will not have the boldness, doors will not be opened, and Christ will not manifest Himself as needed. Satan laughs at prayerless warriors. John Piper's statement is powerful:

> *Life is war. That's not all it is. But it is always that . . .*
> *But most people do not believe this in their hearts. Most*
> *people show by their priorities and their casual approach to*
> *spiritual things that they believe we are in peacetime, not*
> *wartime.*
>
> *Very few people think that we are in a war that is greater*
> *than World War II, or than any imaginable nuclear war.*
> *Few reckon that Satan is a much worse enemy than any*
> *earthly foe, or realize that the conflict is not restricted to*
> *any one global theater, but is in every town and city in the*
> *world.*
>
> *Who considers that the casualties of this war do not merely*
> *lose an arm or an eye or an earthly life, but lose everything,*
> *even their own souls, and enter a hell of everlasting*
> *torment? Until we feel the force of this, we will not pray as*
> *we ought. We will not even know what prayer is . . .*
>
> *Prayer is the communication with headquarters by which*
> *the weapons of warfare are deployed according to the will*
> *of God . . . Prayer is the walkie-talkie of the church on the*
> *battlefield of the world in the service of the word. It is not a*
> *domestic intercom to increase the temporal comforts of the*
> *saints. It malfunctions in the hands of soldiers who have*
> *gone AWOL. It is for those on active duty. And in their*
> *hands it proves the supremacy of God in the pursuit of the*
> *nations.*
>
> *When missions move forward by prayer it magnifies the*
> *power of God. When it moves by human management it*
> *magnifies man.*[6]

What would such extraordinary, wartime prayer for lost people look like? A few years ago I mentioned in a message in Reno, Nevada, the need for us to pray unceasingly for the lost. A year later I returned to the same city, and a man came up to me after the service.

"When you preached last year," he said, I realized to my shame that to my best of my knowledge, I had never really prayed for lost men. I asked God to bring unbelievers across my path that I could intercede for them."

"I am now praying," he said with tears, "for seventy lost men every day." I wonder what would happen if every church was filled with such intercessors!

Constant Intentionality

One of the most effective disciples of Christ I've ever known lived in Norman, Oklahoma, and was a member of the church I pastored. Wayne earned his living selling metal buildings, but his occupation was to serve Christ by seeking and saving those far from God.

This was his method of evangelism: Every morning he reminded himself in prayer of his calling. As he waited on customers throughout the day he would pray, "Lord, I'm reporting for duty. If this is a person you want to introduce to Yourself, then open the conversation and give me the words I need."

That's it. Then he'd wait on the Lord's promptings and go through the doors the Lord would open. Invariably, his customer would ask some question or share some need that gave Wayne the opportunity to share his story of how He came to Christ and the change it had made in his life.

"Lord, I'm reporting for duty."

Wayne always had his spiritual antenna up because he knew that was his main job: to seek and to save the lost.

I can't count the number of times he called and said, "Bill, do you have a minute to come over to my office? I want to introduce you to my new friend who has just given his life to Christ!"

There was a difference about Wayne. He lived for Christ. That was all he really cared about. And God knew it and consistently funneled lost people in Wayne's direction. There was a unique sense of God's presence about Wayne because he was wholeheartedly engaged in the prime initiative.

We must help our people see the opportunities all around them. Peter reminded his hearers we are "aliens, scattered" (1 Peter 1:1). An alien is a stranger in a foreign land. And "scattered" is an agricultural term that means to be sown like seed. If you were to place on the wall a map of your city, pinpointed by each neighborhood and business where the people in your church live and work, you would see the reality of Peter's description. God has placed us among people who need His Son.

We should be like battlefield strategists who understand that God has graciously placed us shoulder-to-shoulder with people who need forgiveness and life. Your grouchy neighbors are not an intrusion to ministry, they are our ministry!

Constant Broadening

If our hearts beat in unison with the Warrior-King's, we will also be led to engage in His work around the world. There is no reason why most followers of Christ cannot go somewhere outside their city every year, for the sake of the gospel. Whether it's "Judea, Samaria, or the uttermost parts of the world" does not matter as long as we go by the Spirit's initiation. Good church leaders will be sensitive to help their people think bigger and engage with different people groups. If our hearts are full of Christ, we will find ourselves not only weeping over Jerusalem, but also engaging the woman at the well in Samaria.

This worldwide passion should also be reflected in our giving and budgeting. For many years, 95 percent of the church resources in the world have been spent on America, with only 5 percent of the world's population. This is horribly imbalanced. And where our treasure is, there is our heart. Financial selfishness provides a telling illustration of a lost sense of mission.

You can't do everything. That's not your responsibility. But you can do what the Spirit prompts. You could begin to grow your missions giving by a certain percentage every year. You could adopt an unreached people group. You could strategically engage: locally, nationally, and internationally. You could go on a mission trip yourself this year.

If you do, you will see Christ manifesting His presence even more clearly. For where His people are engaged in His mission, Christ uniquely makes Himself known.

Constant Multiplication

Over the past several years we have edited our church's mission statement three times. It first read, "We exist to cooperate with God in developing fully devoted followers of Jesus Christ." We realized only God can save and we must cooperate with Him. But after awhile, we realized that the goal of our church was not merely to see a few individuals come to Christ.

Heaven is a community of believers and our church should be a microcosmic picture of eternity. So, we changed it to read," We exist to cooperate with God in developing a *community* of fully devoted followers of Jesus Christ." But after a few years we had another thought. Our goal should not be to simply develop one church in one location. We should not be satisfied with "Us Four and No More" found in many churches. We should be interested in church planting. This moves the mission from addition to multiplication and makes the rapid increase of the kingdom a reality.

Our current statement says this: "We exist to cooperate with God in developing *multiplying* communities of fully devoted followers of Jesus Christ."

This Biblical perspective has changed everything. We realize our church is not just about our church. Our mission is to plant churches in Jerusalem, Judea, Samaria, and around the world, who will do the same. Every mission trip is not just a trip, but an opportunity to help plant a multiplying church. Everything is focused on this multiplying pattern.

If you want to see a continually growing movement you must understand and build a culture of multiplication.

It is not easy, but when your church catches this vision it is strategic and powerful. If you want to see a continually growing movement you must understand and build a culture of multiplication.

For instance, every believer must not just disciple others, but see discipling's end goal as building a disciplemaker. This is multiplication, not addition. And the results of this are staggering.

This means the goal of every small group is not just a good group, but raising up apprentices in the group who will multiply small groups. The goal of church planting is not just planting another congregation, but developing another multiplying, church planting church that will become a church planting center.

This Biblical principle, once permeating the thinking of each believer and each group and each church, creates a movement mentality that is exponential in his growth and limitless in its possibilities.

Much has been written on a church planting philosophy, so I will not elaborate here. The expansion of this thought will be left to others books. But the last few paragraphs may be the most important you will read in this entire chapter!

Constant Celebration

More than almost anything, regularly hearing the stories of changed lives and the multiplying movement of God will motivate mission. There's nothing more valuable than a simple testimony—shared live, by video, or in print. Healthy churches are stirred by life-changing stories.

The *esprit de corps* of military troops can boost their effectiveness. The stories of their heroes—reminding them their cause is winnable—encourage them to boldness.

Baptisms provide a great opportunity to celebrate and hear, once again, that Jesus is fulfilling the task for which He came and using people in the process. Surround the baptismal pool with the people who have helped that person come to Christ. Let the church rejoice not only in the new life in Christ, but also in believers who are fulfilling their mission. Use this moment to remind the congregation of the glorious reason we are left on this earth.

THE MOST UNLIKELY PLACE

Some of the greatest opportunities for witness come during times of stress or suffering. We resist them, but often they are designed by God so those around us may see the sufficiency of the Christ who lives within us. We should stay alert to these moments, for no situation is a limit to evangelism. Life's harder moments often bring our greatest opportunities. Look for the unforeseen openings to share the reason for the "hope that is in you" (1 Peter 3:15).

Paul wrote the book of Philippians from a Roman prison cell. This was no jail like we know now, complete with exercise facilities and cafeteria. But for Paul, the setting was immaterial. A jail cell was simply one more platform for the gospel.

> *Now I want you to know, brethren, that my circumstances*
> *have turned out for the greater progress of the gospel, so*
> *that my imprisonment in the cause of Christ has become*
> *well known throughout the whole praetorian guard and to*
> *everyone else, and that most of the brethren, trusting in the*
> *Lord because of my imprisonment, have far more courage*
> *to speak the word of God without fear.*
> *(Philippians 1:12–14)*

Lost people were seeing the light, and believers were joining the fight! We see in the next verses why this so thrilled Paul's heart. Why he was not feverishly writing his congressman to get him out of this undeserved suffering. Read on:

> *Yes, and I will rejoice, for I know that this will turn out for*
> *my deliverance through your prayers and the provision*
> *of the Spirit of Jesus Christ, according to my earnest*
> *expectation and hope, that I will not be put to shame in*
> *anything, but that with all boldness, Christ will even*
> *now, as always, be exalted in my body, whether by life or*
> *by death. For to me, to live is Christ and to die is gain.*
> *(Philippians 1:18–21)*

I don't believe Paul ever knew or cared if he would get out of prison. He understood something greater. He knew he could enjoy spiritual deliverance: the ability to live joyfully and fruitfully in any circumstance. Such a man is truly free.

Paul knew this deliverance would occur because of the believers' "prayers and the provision of the Spirit of Jesus Christ." He knew God answered prayer—and that the Christ in him would be sufficient, whatever came. But there was one more key ingredient that made Paul so effective and even joyful in suffering: *He had settled the issue of why he lived.*

He wasn't living for comfort, prestige, or pleasure. He was beyond that. His Savior had delivered Him eternally and Paul lived for Christ to be seen in and through his mortal body. If Christ's presence could be more visible, resulting in more people coming to faith, then Paul would embrace any suffering to see that accomplished.

Is that your perspective in your difficulties? Do you see the Divine perspective on where you are? Do you realize the sufficiency of the "provision of the Spirit of Jesus Christ"? Are you enlisting people to pray for you and trusting it will be enough?

Have you settled the issue of why you live? Do you realize the whole purpose of what you're experiencing may be so the world would hear an undeniable witness of Christ's sufficiency? Your problems may not be a hindrance, but your greatest platform for your mission to seek and to save the lost. Every experience can be a platform for witness to a watching world.

THE LIGHT BULB PARABLE

Once there was a little light bulb that lived at the local store. His days were mundane and long, so he decided he wanted to discover the meaning and purpose of his life. He hopped off the shelf and wandered down the street.

Soon he entered a massive market. He saw rows and rows of vegetables and fruits. There were apples and oranges, bananas and melons. Every shape and size and color. Then he saw an onion.

"That's it!" he cried. "I'll climb up in the case and be an onion."

But soon he realized he would be tasteless in that role.

So he wandered down the street. Looking up, he noticed a doorknob.

"Eureka! I can be a doorknob. How wonderful to help people go in and out. To help them get where they need to go!"

Then, to his chagrin, he realized he just couldn't handle it!

Wandering on, he came to an ice cream store. He stood at the window for a long time watching the children, laughing as the cold ice cream ran down their chins.

"Hallelujah," he shouted. "What a joy! I know my destiny! I'll hop up inside a cone and be an ice cream dip! What a delight to give these children such joy!"

Then, to his dismay, he remembered that he just couldn't lick it.

Then he came upon a baseball field. He saw the children running and playing and the ball soaring across the field.

"At last!" he exclaimed. "I've found it. I'll be a baseball!"

Then he quickly realized it might be a . . . shattering experience.

Dejected and dismayed, the little light bulb stumbled into a store at dusk and lay down, weary from his journey.

Suddenly the room was filled with brilliance. He looked up and on the ceiling were hundreds of lights. Little lights and big lights; lights with crystal hanging from their arms and some with wide blades swirling around their heads. He was awestruck.

A big, daddy light looked down at the little light bulb. "What are you doing?"

"I'm trying to find my meaning and purpose in life," the little light bulb said. "I want to know why I exist."

"You dim-watt!" said the big, daddy light. "Don't you know you were created for one purpose? You were made to give light!" And he plugged the little bulb into a socket.

Suddenly the light bulb felt the power coursing through his little light bulb veins. What a thrill to express the light through his unique shape and design! And, most importantly, to do exactly what he was created to do!

Through the years, the little light bulb was plugged into many different sockets. But he discovered it didn't matter where he was placed. He could fulfill his purpose and give light wherever he was.

And to his amazement, he even discovered that the darker the darkness around him, the more brilliant his light became!

THE ENDGAME

The great mission of every believer and every church is to lead people to Christ for the glory of God. We are not designed to introduce them to a program or a manner of living, but to vibrant, living Savior. We are to walk them into His presence so their lives can connect to Him.

The more we lead our church to engage in this mission, the more we will experience the sweet fragrance of Christ's presence everywhere around us. God manifests Himself most greatly when we join Him in what He came to accomplish!

1. Stephen Olford, The Secret of Soul-Winning, (Chicago: Moody Press, 1963), 35.

2. C.S. Lewis, The Weight of Glory, (New York: The MacMillan Co., 1949), 14–15.

3. Stephen Olford, The Secret of Soul-Winning, (Chicago: Moody Press, 1963), 9.

4. Olford, 10–11.

5. J.H. Jowett, The Passion for Souls, (New York: Fleming Revell, 1905), 90–91.

6. John Piper, Let the Nations Be Glad, (Grand Rapids, Mich.: Baker Academic, 2010), 41–45.

9

PRAY UNCEASINGLY

> *"The one concern of the devil is to keep Christians from praying. He fears nothing from prayerless studies, prayerless work, and prayerless religion. He laughs at our toil, mocks at our wisdom, but trembles when we pray."[1]*
>
> *Samuel Chadwick*

If I gave you money to build a new home, you would soon realize it was not enough! You would go to your builder and delete a room or two, maybe three. Honestly, almost any room could be removed and life could continue. It might create some difficulty, but you could survive. But one virtually unseen part of your house is indispensible. If the foundation were not there, everything would collapse. The first big rain would shift the house and crack the walls. Soon, all you had invested would be lost.

Sadly, it has taken me over forty years of ministry to realize this, but the following thought changed everything for me: Prayer is not a side room of the church, but the foundation. The church in our nation has lost this foundation—the bedrock of humble, repentant, fervent prayer.

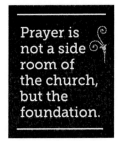

Prayer is not a side room of the church, but the foundation.

Often we list the various components of church life such as preaching, worship, community, Bible study, and giving. And the end of this list—the very end—would be prayer. Prayer is a small"ministry"of the church that few are interested in. We nod that prayer is important, but our daily experience indicates what we really think. Tragically, only 5 percent of churches in America have any consistent, strategic prayer ministry. Out of sight, out of mind.

"My wife is the pray-er," one old buzzard said to me with a laugh in one of my early churches.

I thought, but had the wisdom not to say: "I guess that's why she's the one who is humble, who is communing with God, who is receiving power and direction and life, who is bringing God into the equation, who is hearing God and walking with God and touching the lives of others. And that may be why you're missing all of that, trying to live life on your own without God and bearing very little fruit."

Not so funny.

Why would God ever make Himself known to one who is not interested in Him? Who couldn't care less what He thinks? Who never has the humility to consult Him? Who for years has shown absolutely no interest in communing? Who does not and will not pray?

If we long for a church where God is pleased to dwell and fill with His presence, we must learn the value and habit of prayer without ceasing. It must become a foundational, driving priority in our church.

AN IRREFUTABLE CONSTANT

When you study the biblical and historical accounts of revival and spiritual awakening, you see many variations. But a few elements are always present. Fervent, united prayer has preceded every major movement of God. As Matthew Henry said, "When God intends great mercy on His people, He always sets His people a'praying."[2]

The extraordinary manifestations of God's presence always come after a return to desperation and dependency, vividly signified by a resurgence of prayer . . . the crying out of the heart and a faith that looks upward. Revival (the presence of God manifested in more visible demonstration) is always birthed in repentant prayer.

> Fervent, united prayer has preceded every major movement of God.

This is a dilemma for most pastors and ministry leaders, for prayer seems our last resort, not our first response. Our self-centered, humanistic Christianity balks at prayer. Until we're in crisis, it seems needless. But it's not just the people. Most studies of pastors' prayer lives report the average is just five to seven minutes a day in concentrated intercession. Before you scoff, tally up the time you spend daily communing with God.

Will this ever change? It must if we long for a Presence-Centered church.

PRAY ABOUT PRAYER

It's so obvious, it's usually overlooked. If God invites us to pray and promises to answer our prayers, and if one of our great concerns (and His) is our lack of prayer, why would we not pray about our prayer life and that of our church? Why not pray about prayer?

Wouldn't God be pleased with such a request? Wouldn't He rejoice that we were finally seeing our foundational need to be in constant communion with Him? Don't you imagine He would rush to our aid and begin to lift our wings in prayer in ways we could never do on our own?

Instead of condemning yourself about your prayerlessness, why not use those moments in simple intercession around one simple, power-packed, prayer from Luke 11:1: "Lord, teach us to pray!" Each word carries meaning.

> ### *LORD,* TEACH US TO PRAY!
> We cannot teach ourselves. We are weak and ignorant about how to commune with You. We need a great Teacher. One who will not give up on us. One who will meet us where we are and lead us where we need to go. There is no One who knows more about the subject than You. So, LORD, teach us to pray!

> ### LORD, *TEACH* US TO PRAY!
> Instruct us. Sit us down daily to learn the ways of prayer. Let us see things about prayer that we have never seen, then experience You in prayer in ways we never dreamed possible. Not only teach me, O, Lord,

but use me to teach others. To help them develop prayer as the foundation of their lives. Lord, TEACH us to pray!

LORD, TEACH *US* TO PRAY!
Let me sit in your classroom and learn of You. Do not pass me by in the school of prayer. May I be the one in my family, my church, my community who knows how to pray. Do not let me rest, O, Lord, until You lift me by Your grace from my lethargy to become a person of unceasing prayer.

And don't stop with me, O, Lord. Teach our church to pray. Teach the church in our city to pray. Set Your people to praying across our nation that we may give You the place You deserve in our affections and service. Lord, teach US to pray!

LORD, TEACH US *TO* PRAY!
Forgive us for our incredible prayerlessness. For the years wasted in humanistic thinking and doing. Forgive us for trying to run without taking the first step in communion with You.

Do whatever is necessary so prayer becomes our first response, not our last resort. Help us realize the value of communion with You and embrace a lifestyle of prayer. Help us pray at all times and not faint. Lord, teach us TO pray!

LORD, TEACH US TO *PRAY!*
Show us what prayer is—and its necessity. Teach us the multiple forms of intercession that unite us to Your heart and invite Your presence. Deliver us from a prayerless life, prayerless homes, and prayerless churches.

Lead us to work, dear Lord, but teach us first, foremost, and fully to PRAY!

Pray about your prayer life. You might be astounded a year from now what God has done. He's very effective at His job. And He has pledged His very nature against His promises. He said He will answer the believing prayers of His children.

And Pray About Your Prayer Meetings

Perhaps because I have died a thousand deaths in boring, lifeless, long prayer meetings, I now find myself crying out to God to show up at these gatherings. To make Himself known. To direct the meeting, for He is a far better prayer leader than any of us. To lead us to the "effective prayers" that will "accomplish much" (James 5:16). God wants our prayer meetings filled with His life and power, and to greatly advance the kingdom.

You can find many great books and tools to aid you in leading prayer. Become a student of prayer. The ways of God in prayer are as varied and creative as God Himself. And do not neglect the use of Scripture. You'll never stand on more solid ground than when you take God's Word, digest it, then turn it into a prayer before Him. Almost any Scripture can be read and applied through prayer. But above all, pray for these meetings.

And Your Leaders

Prayer should begin with the leaders. If you and other leaders are not regularly praying, ask God to help you begin. Set aside time to pray together. Make it an unyielding priority. If you're not good at it, if prayer is stilted, then pray about these prayer times. Become equipped to lead your leaders better. Don't let these critical moments digress into mere discussions. Sacrifice everything to actually pray.

As you begin, read the Word out loud together and hear what "the Spirit is saying to the churches," then spend time praying-in these truths. Ask God to make these the church's most powerful prayer seasons, because these moments are discipling your leaders to lead others in prayer. Help them learn not only the priority of prayer, but the process.

Years ago I realized that if we were to have a praying church, our staff must lead the way. It took time and intentionality, but now our weekly staff prayer meeting is the most important meeting of our week. We schedule nothing behind this hour of prayer so that if God desires to expand it, He has that freedom.

Our Elder team also spends large amounts of time praying together. These times, plus our weekly men's and women's prayer gatherings, are the foundation supporting our church. This is where we mutually disciple our leadership as we bring God into every facet of church life.

Take prayer retreats together. Teach on prayer. Do whatever is necessary to develop leaders who lead in prayer—and who are leading the leaders in their area of ministry to pray.

And the Number of Intercessors
One more important suggestion: Ask God to give you committed prayer warriors. Several years ago, I grew discouraged by the small numbers in some of our prayer gatherings. We had seen God move in the past. Many of our people understand the need for prayer, but their numbers were waning.

The Lord laid a number on my mind. I began to ask Him for that number of intercessors. I wanted to develop a "program" to make this happen, but the Lord told me to simply pray. Within the year, in some ways I would have never dreamed possible, God gave us that many intercessors—faithful men and women who would come when called and knew how to lay hold of heaven.

Now God is leading me to ask for more! It seems like the kind of request He would love to answer.

Don't be discouraged with smaller numbers. Intercessors are your Special Forces. I would rather have twenty people who really knew how to move heaven than 200 people with insincere hearts, simply mouthing words. But expect the numbers to grow. As your people see key leaders grasp the joy of prayer and the necessity of intercession to accelerate the accomplishment of the mission, it will become contagious. Ask God to spread a passion for intercession like a fast-moving virus among your people!

DEVELOP A RHYTHM OF PRAYER
We must start somewhere. We must begin in our own closet, then seek to build concentric circles, pulling people closer and closer to the heart of God. You might be surprised to discover there are more people than you realize interested in the right kind of prayer.

As Christian leaders, we should be our church's greatest experts on prayer. Our job, after all is "prayer and the ministry of the word" (Acts 6:4). Notice the order of those two elements. We will be surprised at how many of the other components of our leadership are automatically resolved as we really pray. If you don't know how to lead a prayer meeting effectively . . . learn! Study the resources available and ask God to teach you.

> **As Christian leaders, we should be our church's greatest experts on prayer.**

Our country's First, Second, and Third Great Awakenings were marked by a wonderful, sustainable prayer pattern that would serve us well to follow. Churches committed themselves to a rhythm of revival praying, often signing covenants. Today, many prayer advocates have adopted this pattern as the National Prayer Accord.[3] Simple and doable by the power of the Spirit, it includes weekly prayer, monthly prayer, quarterly prayer, and annual prayer.

Weekly Prayer

Teach your people to pray at least once a week for the manifest presence of God to descend upon your church. Before the First and Second Great Awakenings, this was usually done on Saturday night as people prayed that God would attend the preaching of His Word. Develop in your people a pattern of prayer so that God would manifest Himself in your weekly worship gatherings. Teach them to come praying as they enter into worship.

Your church may already have regularly scheduled weekday prayer times. Push them to make sure they are praying for God to manifest Himself in His body, the church. Teach them to pray for a Presence-Centered church.

Monthly Prayer

Devote at least one meeting a month to churchwide prayer for God's presence. Pray for all that is happening in the coming month. Pray through Scripture. Vary your prayer between private prayers, groups of three to four, and the entire group. Pray much about these prayer gatherings. Have your best prayer leaders (which should be your pastors) lead these times. Many churches pray on the first Monday of every month.

Don't be discouraged by small numbers. Concentrate on effectiveness in prayer, then ask God to grow the number of intercessors.

Quarterly Prayer

God is uniquely drawn to united prayer. In Scripture we see that every time the people humbly united in prayer God always responded with His presence.

God is uniquely drawn to united prayer.

Covenant to pray with other congregations. There is one church in your city and we should be acknowledging and praying with each other. "All the house of Israel lamented [cried out] after the Lord" (1 Samuel 7:2 *emphasis added*). This takes time to develop. Begin by inviting one or two other pastors to have their congregations join you in a First-Monday prayer meeting on a quarterly basis. Fill this session with worship and prayer. How awesome it would be, in time, to see the whole church in your city unite in quarterly prayer!

For more encouragement and instruction on how to develop citywide, unified prayer read *OneCry: A Nationwide Call for Spiritual Awakening*[4] At www.OneCry.com website, you can also download several helps including the e-book *Inviting God's Manifest Presence to Your City*.[5] You'll find detailed instructions on how to foster united prayer in your city.

Annual Prayer

It's vital to call our congregations to join with God's church across the nation in prayer for national spiritual awakening. The first Thursday in May in the United States has been wonderfully given for this purpose. Each year, tens of thousands of prayer gatherings are held on this day.

Every time in human history when all of God's people have united in humble, repentant prayer, God has answered. We may think we're waiting for God to send awakening to our nation. Perhaps, as we see in 2 Chronicles 7:14, God is waiting for us to humble ourselves and pray, seek His face, and turn from our wicked ways!

PRAYER WITH NO INTERMISSION

It seems impossible. In the middle of Paul's admonitions to the Thessalonians he gives a simple, three-word command: "Pray without ceasing" (1 Thessalonians 5:17). Most think this is unattainable, but these words form life's most important door.

Prayer means being with Him. It implies humility, for in real prayer we turn to a Source beyond ourselves. Think of the publican beating his chest and groaning for God (Luke 18:13). Prayer is a solemn recognition that you need Someone . . . for fellowship, instruction, power, help, life, and mission.

God Is Calling

All of life is a process for God to restore what was lost in Eden (and more). God is bringing us back to Himself. The whole work of Christ is aimed at this blessed reality. When we realize this and are drawn to Him by grace, we are saved from sin and death and hell.

But salvation includes so much more than this legal pardon. It opens the way for an ongoing relationship. Prayer is how this unceasing exchange is designed to occur. Prayer is meant to be a running dialogue with the God of the universe who loves us with perfect, unceasing passion. Prayer is not merely something we "do" as a follower of Christ. It should be the atmosphere in which we now live, the air we breathe.

We must realize that prayer is not just about us. It is also for Him. Just as you long to be with your earthly family, the Father wants to be with His children.

God Is Working

There are things God plans to do through no other means but prayer. He reminds us of this continually to bring us back into constant communion with Him. He not only invites us, He also makes outlandish promises: "All things you ask in prayer, believing, you will receive" (Matthew 21:22). "The effective prayer of a righteous man can accomplish much" (James 5:16). It sounds too amazing to be true, but it is the cry of a Father intent upon bringing us to Himself. He lovingly places this limitation on our life to make sure we live together with Him.

> There are things God plans to do through no other means but prayer.

But prayer without ceasing? This is the fantastical part. We can imagine ourselves praying occasionally . . . when there is an urgent need ... when we need divine paramedics to rush to our aid. But without ceasing? With no intermission?

God Is Present

God is here. You can leave your receiver tuned to Him constantly and hear the dialogue of His love, encouragement, and direction. To go there means you must set aside other voices and distractions and give Him your attention. You must silence every idol: each loud, competing voice. God is there, but you will not hear Him unless you refuse the noise around you.

Do whatever is necessary to listen. You must pray, not just with a bowed head or bended knee, but with a heart unceasingly tuned to Him throughout every moment. Prayer is not a part of the Christ-life; it is the Christ-life, and you must sacrifice everything to still each competing voice.

> Prayer is not a part of the Christ-life; it is the Christ-life, and you must sacrifice everything to still each competing voice.

If you do, you will find the sweetest, most intimate words a human can experience. You will be surprised at its refreshment and joy, amazed at its consistency. Stunned that it is so personal. Humbled by the depth of His genuine love and the intimacies of that expression. Awed by how perfectly God knows exactly what you need to hear every second of the day. And you will wonder why you waited so long to pray without ceasing.

1. http://christian-quotes.ochristian.com/Samuel-Chadwick-Quotes/page-3.shtml.
2. Matthew Henry, quoted by Arthur Wallis, In the Day of Thy Power, (London: Christian Literature Crusade, 1956), 112.
3. www.prayerconnect.net/resources/prayer-accord.
4. Byron Paulus and Bill Elliff, OneCry: A Nationwide Call for Spiritual Awakening, (Chicago: Moody Publishers, 2014).
5. http://onecry.com/wp-content/uploads/2015/05/Ebook-revised-3-9-15.pdf.

10

GREATER THINGS

John Scully was an amazing businessman. He became the youngest CEO ever to lead the Pepsi Corporation.

One day a young, entrepreneurial business leader approached Scully with an audacious request. He invited him to leave his prestigious position and join a fledgling computer company named after a fruit. Steve Jobs pushed and pulled on Scully for an answer.

Scully said he thought deeply about the decision, but it was Job's final question that caused him to join Apple.

> *"Do you want to spend the rest of your life selling sugared water or do you want to come with us and change the world?"*

What will it be for you? Do you want to spend the rest of your life on a path that leads only to human results? A life that can be explained in terms of your ability? A life of just you?

Christ offers more. He said His children would be able to do greater things than He accomplished (John 14:12). Not greater in significance, but greater in scope. He filled His followers with Himself and cast them like seed around the world to bring a great harvest.

That includes you. It's all possible when we live with a passion for His presence: in our lives, the life of our church, and the lives of those around us . . . *because everything flows from the presence of the Lord.*

My great-grandmother was a simple farm wife. She and her young husband left eastern Tennessee to build a home in the Oklahoma Territory. Life was hard and my great grandmother became deathly ill. She pled with her husband to not let her die in "this wild Indian territory." He sold the farm and they boarded a train in Fort Smith, Arkansas, to head home. They changed trains in Little Rock and soon realized she would not last much longer. They laid her out on a train seat. She called her husband to her side, and he knelt beside her. She was a follower of Christ, but her husband was an unbeliever.

"I want you to promise me two things," she said. "One, that you'll give your life to Christ. And two, that you'll raise our daughter for Christ."

Then she died.

My great-grandfather's testimony was that he "stayed on his knees a long time and got up a Christian." He went home, buried his wife, and with his infant daughter in his arms, stood at the church and confessed his faith in Christ.

He later married a Christian woman and they had several children. One was my grandfather, who became a pastor.

My grandfather had a boy and a girl. The boy, my father, became a pastor. Dad and Mom had four children. The three boys all became pastors, and my sister married a pastor. The four of us have had eighteen children. At this point, thirteen are either pastors or missionaries, married to a pastor or missionary, or preparing for ministry.

All this came from one woman who experienced God's presence and helped her husband come to know the Christ she loved.

My great-grandmother probably died thinking her life a failure—that she couldn't even lead her own husband to faith. But the presence of God through her life changed all of that. Only eternity will record the legacy she left for Christ.

This story always challenges me to remember: God wants to use every one of us—more than we can imagine. He can change the trajectory of entire generations.

God has more for you—and for the church where you are planted. Don't underestimate what He can do with anyone who is willing to let Him be in charge. But remember, everything flows from the presence of the Lord.

Why not join Him . . . *and change the world?*

APPENDIX A

Chapter Discussion Questions

Chapter 1: The Door

1. What does the statement, "Everything flows from the presence of the Lord," mean to you?

2. How important is that statement to your life and ministry? To the life of your church?

3. On a scale of 1-10 (10 being best) how much do you sense your church is driven by a desire for the presence of God?

4. Where is God most present in your church? What environments or areas?

5. If you are a leader:
   a. How greatly do you hunger for God's presence?
   b. Would others say that your life and ministry is saturated with the presence of God?

6. Are you experiencing God's presence individually? Corporately as a church?

7. How important is it at this time for us to see a Divine outpouring of God's presence in nationwide revival?

Chapter 2: Enter First

1. Is Mark 3:14-15 your view of discipleship? Why or why not? How would your life change if this were your view?

2. What will happen if a leader is not experiencing God's presence daily? How important is this?

3. There are multiple ways to experience and cultivate the presence of God in your life. Evaluate, on a scale of 1-10, how you are doing in seeking God's presence through the following means:
   a. Daily time
   b. Extended time
   c. Fasting
   d. Unceasing prayer
   e. Spiritual Examination
   f. Honest Accountability
   g. United prayer

4. Which of these areas needs the most attention?

5. What are the immediate steps you can take in these areas, or the most needed areas, to begin to seek the presence of Christ more fully in your life?

Chapter 3: Listen Up

1. How important is it to understand the ways of God?

2. What could/should you do to more fully understand the ways of God, so that you could better cooperate with Him?

3. What steps can you take to live and lead, as a leader or as a church, making plans that are God-initiated?

4. How important is prayer to God-initiation?

5. When was the last time God interrupted your plans, desiring to take you in a new direction, and you seized the Divine moment and cooperated with Him? What were the results?

6. Do you think your church quenches the Spirit? Do you quench the Spirit? What could change this?

Chapter 4: Remove Barriers

1. Do you take time regularly to evaluate where the spiritual bunkers are in your church? If not, what steps can you take to go there?

2. What are the "heart barriers" in your church? (Think deeply about this question for much depends upon seeing and addressing these bunkers).

3. Are you discipling the willing people in your church?

4. Are you willing to confront, as needed, the issues that are hindering the life of your church?

5. Where are the structural or methodological bunkers in your church?

6. Honestly think through and discuss the 4 Wineskin questions.
   a. Is there anything in my life or our church that I am unwilling to change so that Christ's presence may be experienced more fully?

   b. Are all our wineskins effective? Are they doing what God intended when they were first developed?

c. Is each of our current wineskins filled with the life of God? Is the wineskin itself aborting God's presence or is something wrong with it that prevents the presence of Christ? What change is needed?

d. Is the life of Christ flowing through the wineskins of our church? Are people inside and outside the church encountering the presence of Christ? Do we see lives changed by the power of God?

Chapter 5: Create Environments

1 Evaluate your life and your church to see if you are creating environments for growth.
   a. One-to-One
   b. The Inner Three
   c. Small groups
   d. The Core
   e. The Congregation
   f. The Crowd

2. Are we helping our people experience the presence of Christ in each of these environments?

3. What is our strongest environment and weakest environment?

4. What changes need to be made to make sure that each of these arenas is filled with the presence of Christ?

Chapter 6: Experience Deeply

1. Are your large gatherings filled with the presence of Christ?

2. If not, what is hindering that? If so, what is helping this?

3. What steps can be taken to more greatly experience Christ's presence in your worship gatherings?

4. (For Pastors and Teachers) Are you doing the necessary work to make sure that your preaching/teaching is helping people encounter Christ? Are you…
   a. Listening?
   b. Prepared?
   c. Filled?
   d. Direct?
   e. Christ-centered?

5. Are you giving the church body appropriate, God-led times to breath? Do the people have opportunity, in appropriate environments, to express themselves, share testimonies, express their gifts? How could this be enhanced?

Chapter 7: Equip Intentionally

1. On a scale of 1-10, how well do you feel you have had opportunity to be equipped?

2. How well is the church doing overall in equipping its people?

3. Is your equipping merely "head" or "hand" knowledge or is it also developing the heart and leading people to know HIM?

4. What additional tools need to be found or developed to equip people intentionally?

5. How would you describe a fully devoted follower of Christ?

6. Do you have a plan to help people get there? To mature people to the "measure of the stature of the fullness of Christ?"

7. Is there a culture of discipleship in your church? If not, what are the areas that need development?

8. Look at the extended sentence on discipleship. What parts of this are missing in your church that needs development?

Chapter 8: Engage Passionately

1. Are you personally, intentionally engaged with people far from God?

2. Is your church aggressively pursuing people far from God?

3. Do you think it is true that "Christ is uniquely present in places where His people are engaged in His mission"? Why or why not?

4. Does your church constantly remind people of this mission?

5. Are you giving the necessary equipping to train people in evangelism? If not, how could you begin to change this?

6. Are you praying for lost people? How could this be enhanced?

7. Is your church a mission-minded church? What are evidences of this?

8. If not, what could be the first steps to change this?

9. Does your church live with a multiplication-mindset?

10. Where are the places where your suffering has become a tool God has used for witnessing to others?

Chapter 9: Pray Unceasingly

1. Be very honest: How do you view prayer, as evidenced by your daily practice?

2. Have you been praying about your prayer life? About the prayer life of your church?

3. Are your leaders praying together systematically and continually? If not, how could this be changed?

4. Are you praying regularly with others?

5. What would it take to develop the rhythm of prayer described in this chapter in your church? Do you think this would be helpful?

6. What would it take for you personally to learn how to pray without ceasing?

APPENDIX B

Not I, But Christ

Lord, bend that proud and stiff-necked "I,"
Help me to bow the neck and die,
Beholding Him on Calvary,
Who bowed His Head for me.

The following are some of the features and manifestations of the Self-life. The Holy Spirit alone can interpret and apply this to your individual case. As you read, examine yourself in the very presence of God. Are you ever conscious of:

A secret spirit of pride, an exalted feeling in view of your success or position; because of your good training or appearance; because of your natural gifts and abilities. An important, independent spirit?

Love of human praise; a secret fondness to be noticed; love of supremacy, drawing attention to self in conversation; a swelling out of self when you have had a free time in speaking or praying?

The stirrings of anger or impatience, which, worst of all, you call nervousness or holy indignation; a touchy, sensitive spirit; a disposition to resent and retaliate when disapproved of or contradicted; a desire to throw sharp, heated flings at another?

Self-will; a stubborn, unteachable spirit; an arguing, talkative spirit; harsh, sarcastic expressions; an unyielding, headstrong disposition; a driving, commanding spirit; a disposition to criticize and pick flaws when set aside and unnoticed; a peevish, fretful spirit; a disposition that loves to be coaxed and humored?

Carnal fear; a man-fearing spirit; a shrinking from reproach and duty; reasoning around your cross; a shrinking from doing your whole duty by those of wealth or position; a fearfulness that someone will offend and drive some prominent person away; a compromising spirit?

A jealous disposition, a secret spirit of envy shut up in your heart; an unpleasant sensation in view of the great prosperity and success of another; a disposition to speak of the faults and failings, rather than the gifts and virtues of those more talented and appreciated than yourself? A dishonest, deceitful disposition; the evading and covering of the truth; the covering up of your real faults; leaving a better impression of yourself than is strictly true; false humility; exaggeration; straining the truth?

Unbelief; a spirit of discouragement in times of pressure and opposition; lack of quietness and confidence in God; lack of faith and trust in God; a disposition to worry and complain in the midst of pain, poverty, or at the dispensations of Divine Providence; an overanxious feeling whether everything will come out all right?

Formality and deadness; lack of concern for lost souls; dryness and indifference?

Selfishness; love of ease; love of money?

These are some of the traits which generally indicate carnality in the heart. By prayer, hold your heart open to the searchlight of God. "Search me, O God, and know my heart: try me, and know my thoughts: and see if there be any wicked way in me" (Psalm 139:23–24). The Holy Spirit will enable you, by confession and faith, to bring your self-life to the death (Romans 8:12–13). Do not patch over, but go to the bottom. It alone will pay.

Oh, to be saved from myself, dear Lord,
Oh, to be lost in Thee;
Oh, that it might be no more I,
But Christ that lives in me.

"Create in me a clean heart, O God;
and renew a right spirit within me"
(Psalm 51:10).

Copyright © Christian Communicators Worldwide Unknown. Permission granted for reproduction in exact form. All other uses require written permission.

Find more free articles at www.BulletinInserts.org, a ministry of Christian Communicators Worldwide: www.CCWtoday.org

APPENDIX C

Fifty Marks of a Man of God

Personal questions from the pastoral epistles for those in Christian leadership.

These questions are for those who care about the quality of their leadership. They can also serve to stimulate and guide aspiring leaders (1 Timothy 3:1). There is nothing light or empty here. Only serious leaders will proceed and gain from the exercise of facing biblical evaluation. Will you treat these questions with the respect, concern, and humility they deserve? Your leadership may depend on it.

The pastoral epistles confront the apathy, moral compromise, and lack of decisiveness often found in Christian leaders. They instruct elders, deacons, and missionaries (such as Timothy and Titus) how to live as examples for all believers to follow.

Use your heart and your pen to evaluate. Write out your thoughts below each question. Contemplate. Pray. Above all, be honest.

1 Timothy 3
1. Are you above reproach? Blameless in every area of life? Do you have a good reputation with those inside and outside the church? (vv. 2, 7)

YES NO

2. Are you a one-woman man? Do you have a single-minded devotion to your wife? Are you overcoming problems of lust and moral impurity? (v. 2)

YES NO

3. Are you temperate, sober, and serious-minded about the things of God? Are you vigilant and watchful about your personal life? (v. 2)

YES NO

4. Are you prudent and sensible? Do you exhibit common sense regarding the basic issues of your life and ministry? (v. 2)

YES NO

5. Are you respectable? Do you handle yourself in an orderly and well-behaved manner, rather than being childish, ill-mannered, and immature? (v. 2)

YES NO

6. Are you given to hospitality? Are you willing to open your heart, home, and material resources to others? Do you serve and minister to the needs of others on a regular basis? (v. 2)

YES NO

7. Are you able to teach the Word to others? Do you look for and take advantage of opportunities to communicate biblical truth to those around you? (v. 2)

YES NO

8. Do you exhibit self-control in matters of food and drink or in practices that could cause others to stumble? (v. 3)

YES NO

9. Are you peaceable and non-combative rather than quick-tempered and argumentative? Are you able to deal with those who contradict you in a gentle, reasonable way? (v. 3)

YES NO

10. Are you free from a contentious spirit? Are you "slow to anger" rather than quarrelsome? Do you seek to avoid strife? (v. 3)

YES NO

11. Are you free from the love of money, covetousness, and greed for gain? Have you avoided undue entanglement in secular money

affairs and over-interest in money, retirement, and the things of this world? (v. 3)

YES NO

12. Do you manage your own household well? Are your children faithful rather than rebellious toward God? Do you handle your children with dignity and in a respectable, commendable way that offers an example to others? (v. 4)

YES NO

13. Are you an established believer? Are you mature in the faith rather than a new convert? (v. 6)

YES NO

14. Are you selfless rather than self-willed? Are you willing to yield your rights rather than insisting on getting your own way? (Titus 1:7)

YES NO

15. Are you a lover of that which is good (good men, good things, good values, etc.)? (Titus 1:8)

YES NO

Titus 1
16. Are you just and fair in all your dealings? Do you have a genuine desire to do what is right and honorable in the sight of others? (v. 8)

YES NO

17. Are you devout? Are you wholly devoted to Christ and willing to be set apart unto Him? (v. 8)

YES NO

18. Are you self-controlled? Do you let Christ reign over your life? Are you able to discipline yourself, apart from externally imposed disciplines? (v.8)

YES NO

1 Timothy 4
19. Are you an example of godliness in your speech? (v. 12)

YES NO

20. Are you an example of godliness in your conduct? (v. 12)

YES NO

21. Are you an example of godliness in your love? (v. 12)

YES NO

22. Are you an example of godliness in your faith? (v. 12)

YES NO

23. Are you an example of godliness in your purity? (v. 12)

YES NO

24. Are you taking pains with, absorbed in, persevering, and making evident progress in the development of godly character? (v. 15)

YES NO

25. Are you taking pains with, absorbed in, persevering, and making evident progress in the development of your teaching? (v. 15)

YES NO

1 Timothy 5
26. Do you treat others with respect rather than reproving them sharply? (v. 1, 2)

YES NO

27. Do you take care of the material and spiritual needs of your own household? (v. 8)

YES NO

1 Timothy 6

28. Are you content with what God has provided? Do you see what God has provided as enough? (v. 6–10)

YES NO

2 Timothy 1

29. Do you maintain a clear conscience? Are you consistently right before God and man? (v. 3; 1 Timothy 1:19)

YES NO

30. Have you overcome a spirit of timidity or a man-fearing spirit? Are you unashamed of the Lord and the Lord's servants? (v. 7, 8)

YES NO

2 Timothy 2

31. Are you personally involved in teaching faithful men who in turn can teach others? Do you exhibit a lifestyle of personal discipleship? (v. 2)

YES NO

32. Are you willing to suffer hardship? Are you willing to do the will of God regardless of the cost? (v. 3)

YES NO

33. Are you preoccupied with Christ rather than the things and interests of the world? Are your priorities aligned with those taught in God's Word? Do you have an eternal perspective? (v. 4)

YES NO

34. Do you "compete according to the rules"? Do you order your life according to biblical principles? (v. 5)

YES NO

35. Are you hard-working and diligent? Are you willing to aggressively tackle any responsibility regardless of its difficulty? (v. 6)

YES NO

36. Do you study the Word of God diligently and handle it accurately? (v. 15)

YES NO

37. Do you avoid worldly and empty chatter? (v. 16)

YES NO

38. Do you consistently cleanse yourself of any impurity of life? Do you flee youthful lusts, and are you pursuing righteousness, purity, and holiness? (v. 21, 22)

YES NO

39. Do you refuse foolish and ignorant speculations that produce quarrels? (v. 23)

YES NO

40. Are you kind to all? (v. 24)

YES NO

41. Are you patient when wronged? (v. 24)

YES NO

42. Do you gently correct those who are in opposition to the truth? (v. 25)

YES NO

2 Timothy 3

43. Do you have a godly perspective on the wickedness of the day in which we live? Do you see clearly the enemies that oppose the things of God? (vv. 1–9)

YES NO

44. Are you teachable? Do you follow the example of godly men? (v. 10)

YES NO

45. Are you faithful in the study and application of the Word of God to equip yourself as a man of God? (vv. 14–16)

YES NO

2 Timothy 4

46. Do you proclaim consistently and faithfully the whole counsel of the Word? (v. 2)

YES NO

47. Are you ready to serve God in season and out of season (at all times, regardless of the circumstances)? (v. 2)

YES NO

48. Are you willing to reprove and rebuke men? Are you unafraid to confront others who stand in opposition? Are you more interested in pleasing God than pleasing men? (v. 2)

YES NO

49. Do you minister to others with great patience and biblical instruction? (v. 2)

YES NO

50. Are you fulfilling faithfully the ministry that God has given you right where you are? (vv. 4–8)

YES NO

Obviously, every person God uses contends daily with sin and weakness. Yet no one can willfully and consistently rebel against God and be the leader God wants. Leadership without spirituality usually ends in a mere show of faked piety. Such leadership is not neutral, but damaging to the body of Christ as it cools other believers' flames of passion for the Lord.

Has God shown you something about yourself you wish were not there? For rebellion and pretense there is only one course of action: repentance. Humble yourself and reject the sin, despising it for the evil it is. If you have sinned against others, confess your sin to as many as your sin or its effect has touched. And where you found weakness, renew spiritual disciplines. But in every consideration, apply faith in God the Sanctifier. It is God who makes you holy and effective!

Memorize verses that speak to your need. Let God's Word search you daily. Ask for help from others who can hold you accountable and give you counsel. Aggressively cooperate with the Holy Spirit, the agent of change in your life. Trust God to broaden your leadership according to a growing foundation of true spirituality. And plead with God to keep you from ever being superficial, vain, and useless as a leader. Ask God to make you a vessel fit for the Master's use.

1. Copyright © 1992 Bill Elliff, Distributed by The Summit Church, 6600 Crystal Hill Road, North Little Rock, Arkansas 72118, www.thesummitchurch.org. Permission for use gladly given if this documentation is included.

Appendix D

The Value of Large and Small Groups

The Value of a Large Group	The Value of the Small Group
1. Communication: is conveyed for the whole body, thus insuring unity of direction, purpose, focus, etc. Communication can happen quickly and be conveyed to the whole church	1. Communication: is personal and intimate; it does not, however, have the opportunity of being overseen directly by church leaders
2. Teaching: can be done by spiritually gifted and called pastors and teachers	2. Teaching: is conveyed in a more informal, application-oriented manner. A gifted teacher may or may not be available
3. Purity of Doctrine: can be maintained by the leaders of the church, which offers greater protection against error	3. Purity of Doctrine: can be discussed but often without the benefit of gifted teachers and overall oversight
4. Celebration: can be experienced by the whole and accomplishes the benefit of helping people feel a part of the great movement	4. Celebration: can be personal and in-depth; more stories are heard; all can participate
5. Evangelism: unbelievers see the value of belief to the whole group, carrying credibility and weight	5. Evangelism: personal conversations can be shared; evangelism through personal ministry can be better accomplished
6. Community: can be experienced minimally at the macro level	6. Community: can be experienced maximally at the micro level
7. The Exercise of Gifts: the spiritual gifts of a few are utilized that are appropriate for the purpose of the gathering	7. The Exercise of Gifts: the spiritual gifts of all in the group can be utilized, although not every gift is usually present
8. Worship: can be led by highly gifted leaders; helps us see the prototype of heaven's gathering, giving the sense of the great movement believers are engaged in	8. Worship: can be experienced through prayer, Word, sharing, and some singing; can be more intimate
9. Giving: can be accomplished to gather resources for the greater advancement of the whole and overseen and dispersed by the elders	9. Giving: can be directed to more specific felt needs of the group and those they are ministering to

Other Writings by Bill Elliff

OneCry!
A Nationwide Call for Spiritual Awakening

(Byron Paulus and Bill Elliff)

WhiteWater
Navigating the Rapids of Church Conflict

Forgiveness
Healing the Harbored Hurts of your Heart

Lifting the Load
How to Gain and Maintain a Clear Conscience

Turning the Tide
Having MORE Kids who Follow Christ

(Holly Elliff with Bill Elliff)

Everyman
the Rescue

50 Marks of a Man of God

Important questions for those in spiritual leadership

Personal Revival Checklist

A spiritual examination from the Sermon on the Mount.

TRUTHINK publications

To order more copies of The Presence-Centered Church or any of our other resources, contact TruthInkPublications@gmail.com

Or visit our website and order at www.thesummitchurch.org
Bulk prices available upon request.